CNN WORLD REPORT
TED TURNER'S INTERNATIONAL NEWS COUP

CNN WORLD REPORT
TED TURNER'S INTERNATIONAL
NEWS COUP

Don M. Flournoy

Director

Institute for Telecommunication Studies,

Ohio University, USA

Acamedia Research Monograph: 9

John Libbey

LONDON · PARIS · ROME

British Library Cataloguing in Publication Data

CNN World Report
Ted Turner's International News Coup
(Acamedia Research Monograph series : 9
I. Title   II. Series
302.23

ISBN: 0 86196 359 8 (Hardback edition)
ISSN: 0956-9057

Series editor: Manuel Alvarado

Published by

John Libbey & Company Ltd, 13 Smiths Yard, Summerley Street,
London SW18 4HR, England
Telephone: 081-947 2777 – Fax: 081-947 2664
John Libbey Eurotext Ltd, 6 rue Blanche, 92120 Montrouge, France
John Libbey - C.I.C. s.r.l., via Lazzaro Spallanzani 11, 00161 Rome, Italy

Printed in Great Britain by Whitstable Litho Ltd, Whitstable, Kent, UK

Contents

Introduction   **1**

Chapter 1   **Cable News Goes Global**   **5**
The *World Report* Experiment   7
The Global Newscast   10
Local News From Abroad   12

Chapter 2   **New Order Journalism**   **17**
Philosophy   17
Rules   25
Staffing   28
Gatekeeping   31
Packaging   34

Chapter 3   **What Makes the News?**   **37**
World Report Content   37
Daily *World Report*   43
World Report Specials   46

Chapter 4   **The Origins of *CNN World Report***   **49**
Information Technologies   49
Regional News Exchanges   51
Training   56
Cable TV and Other Outlets   57
Consumer Interest   59
Profitability   61
International Politics   64
Public Diplomacy   67
Turner Unorthodoxy   68

Chapter 5 **How TV News Organizations See** *World Report*   **71**
Global Audience   71
News Exchange   74
Uncensored Reports   75
Broadcaster Concerns   78
International Usage   79

Chapter 6 **Expanding the World News Agenda**   **83**
Television Diplomacy   84
Alternative News   86
Reciprocal News   88
Inclusive News   89

Chapter 7 **Conclusions**   **93**

INTRODUCTION

It was midnight on a Monday, 26 October 1987. I was flat on my back in the hospital recovering from a lumbar laminectomy (disc surgery) and wide awake from a pain killer intended to help me sleep.

What I caught quite by accident was the inauguration of one of CNN's new international newscasts, without doubt the most striking assortment of news items I had ever seen strung together. What made it unique was that it consisted of a two-hour package of 'unedited and uncensored' local news from around the world reported by local journalists.

I counted at least thirty countries contributing material, all of it collected, packaged and redistributed out of Atlanta, Georgia. I was getting it in Columbus, Ohio, about the same time it was being distributed across six continents.

There were news items from Zimbabwe, Thailand, Venezuela, Poland, Guam, Grenada, Switzerland, Portugal and Cyprus – places you only hear about in America if there is some disaster, an earthquake or a terrorist bomb, a US invasion, or a visit from the US Secretary of State.

Quite a bit of it indeed was of crises and politics. Nepal sent news of its latest flood. A water contamination problem was offered from Puerto Rico. Both of these were covered, in English, by local reporters. In the Zimbabwe piece we saw the laid-out bodies of slain poachers in a local game preserve. Denmark gave us a story about a German ship burning waste at sea being boarded by Green Peace. A contribution by Australia pictured a confrontation between protesters and police at a military installation. Bermuda depicted a crack-down on tax-evaders and Venezuela a crack-down on drug traffickers.

But there were softer items: a horse auction in Poland, beautifully shot using only the natural sound; coverage of a teenage queen contest in American Samoa; a story on children's fashions in Cuba; elections reports in Switzerland and the Bahamas and a story about a whale hunt in St.Vincent and the Grenadines.

Some items resembled the news you often see when you are in a Third World country, 'development communication' news, such as the opening of the new airport in Brunei, a fish breeding operation in Czechoslovakia, celebration of Commonwealth status for Guam and a procession of royal barges on a river in Thailand.

To accomplish this feat, CNN had gone a big step beyond regional satellite news exchange. This was not just a matter of local stations collecting and contributing the news they deemed worthy of wider distribution to a national network. Nor was it a parallel and competitive service to the regional services of neighbouring states, such as Eurovision, Intervision and Asiavision, which operated within geographic and political borders. It was the first truely planetary newscast to which any country in any part of the globe was free to contribute and use as it will.

By 1992, some 10,000 of these local news items had been aired on the *CNN World Report*. Originating from a total of 185 news organizations representing 130 countries, this level of participation without doubt makes *World Report* the most broadly representative newscast ever put together. And with CNN's internationally-distributed satellite signal within reach of 98 per cent of the World's population, it also makes it the world's most widely distributed newscast.

What is also noteworthy about this newscast is that it is the basis for the first truely international news exchange. *CNN World Report* gives broadcasters from Abu Dhabi to Zimbabwe, from Armenia to Uruguay a chance to speak directly to the rest of the world, but of perhaps more lasting consequence is the regular access it gives local stations to international news and views not assembled by the established players, such as World Television News, Visnews, BBC World Service Television and CNN.

CNN World Report: Ted Turner's international news coup is the product of research undertaken by the Institute for Telecommunications Studies at Ohio University to document, analyse and report on this unusual news programme. The book addresses such questions as who contributes to *World Report*? Why do they bother? And what local use is made of *World Report* news? What sort of news is it? How does it compare with the internationally-distributed news of the more established players?

The book also looks at the origins of the *CNN World Report*, especially the way *World Report* draws on the experience base put in place by the broadcasting unions and their regional satellite news exchanges in Eastern Europe, Asia, the Middle East and the Caribbean. It looks at the informal non-contractual agreements which have served as the rules of the exchange, and at the motivations of CNN founder, Ted Turner.

In 1990, Ted Turner told a radio-television news directors conference, 'There will not be a totalitarian state on the planet in 10 years due to communications'. If that prediction turns out to be true, part of the reason will be CNN and its *World Report*. Turner is often featured in the news as a successful capitalist and an entreprenuer, but there is another side of Turner which wants to be even better-known as a man with a social conscience and agenda, one who works for greater international peace and understanding. *World Report*, Turner says, was not created with the intention of making money. It was created for the specific purpose of giving people around the world 'a chance to be heard from'.

In this research, I am especially grateful for the contributions of my Ohio University colleague Robert K. Stewart and students Rani Dilawari, Chuck Ganzert, Chris Friedman, Elizabeth Lozano, Maria Gomez-Murphy, Chun-il Park and Sig-Britt Sandh. At CNN, there are too many to acknowledge, but at the top of the list must be *World Report*'s founding editor-in-chief, Stuart Loory, and his associate producer, Brook McDonald, whose openness to and appreciation for academic research made this investigation possible.

I must also mention *World Report*'s Gerri Anderson, Nicole Couture, Lou Curles, Siobhan Darrow, Jody Hassett, Donna Mastrangelo, Katrina McMillan, Octavia Nasr, Kim Norgaard, Nancy Peckenham, Miriam Pena, Henry Schuster, Tracey Scruggs, Mark Smith, Lori Waffenschmidt and Magda Walter. Ralph Wenge, CNN anchor, Eason Jordan, international news vice president and senior vice president, Bob Furnad, always had an open door for me. Finally, I want to thank my son, Eli, whose careful journals and formal studies during two internships with *World Report* while a student at Indiana University, and whose current position as a Headline News writer, have helped me understand so complex an organization as CNN.

Don M. Flournoy
Director, Institute for Telecommunications Studies
Ohio University, USA

August, 1992

3

Chapter 1   CABLE NEWS GOES GLOBAL

'Diplomats and world leaders are well-served when they ask themselves about how their actions – taken in private tonight – look when reported globally tomorrow on CNN'.

Thomas Johnson, President Cable News Network

During the war of the Persian Gulf, competition was fierce for coverage among television news agencies. US network executives, finding that CNN had the jump on them, complained that CNN received preferential treatment from the Iraqis. CNN journalists maintained open communication channels to the outside throughout most of the war, even after the network news crews had departed Baghdad. A private telephone line for CNN's exclusive use had been arranged in advance with the help of Iraqi officials. Network sources said the Iraqi government had refused to provide the same to ABC, CBS and NBC.

In an *Electronic Media* article entitled 'CNN Grabs Spotlight in Live TV War,' CBS's Washington bureau chief, Barbara Cohen, was reported to have acknowledged that Iraqi leaders regularly viewed CNN, not ABC, CBS or NBC. 'If you're the ministry of information,' she said, 'maybe that's who you do a favour for'.[1] Ironically the Turner organization was instrumental in helping CBS get correspondent Bob Simon and his crew released unharmed after being captured by the Iraqi military.

There is more to this story than meets the eye. CNN began a working relationship with Iraq several years earlier, long before Iraqi leaders began regularly looking to CNN as a source for news. In the Fall of 1987, CNN invited Iraqi Television, along with other Third World broadcasters, to submit items of news and perspectives from its own point of view. CNN promised to carry those items unedited and uncensored in a special weekly segment called *World Report*. The only requirement was that the news items be no longer than three minutes in length and reported in English.

In May 1989, the Director General of Iraqi TV, the Director of News and Current Affairs and the Secretary of the National Planning Committee of Iraq came to the first *CNN World Report* Contributors Conference hosted by Turner Broadcasting in Atlanta. Attending that meeting were about 200 television newscasters and executives from private, public and government agencies representing all regions of the world, including Afghanistan, Australia, Bahamas, Brazil, Colombia, China, Ghana, Haiti, Hungary, Kuwait, Philippines, South Africa and the USSR.

CNN founder R.E. 'Ted' Turner, who footed the bill for the lavish five-day affair and served as host, used the opportunity to talk about 'what we, together, can do to improve the flow of information around the world' and 'what other things we global broadcasters can do that can be of benefit to each other and of benefit to our little planet'.

Cable News Network had been established by Turner as a news programming service for the US cable companies. When CNN went on the air in June 1980, its newscast reached less than two million homes. It was a US$20 million investment which took five years to show the first signs of profit. By 1991, CNN and CNN Headline News were budgeted at US$230 million, contributing 28 per cent of Turner Broadcasting's overall US$1.1 billion in revenues. In the words of Ted Turner, 'I don't think there is any question that we are the World's number one provider of television news'.[2] This is not just boasting. CNN's 24-hour cable news is now the most watched of all the cable services, received by 58 million US homes and, by satellite, in 140 countries. CNN operates 27 news bureaus, nine in the USA and 18 in international locations, with a 1800 person staff.

Events in China at the time of Tiananmen Square, the Persian Gulf war and political changes in South Africa, Eastern Europe and the USSR have helped to solidify CNN's reputation as an international news service, when CNN demonstrated willingness to go after the news and showed it could deliver breaking stories almost as they happened. Although CNN has been praised for its even-handed treatment of the news, it has had its detractors, including those from the USA upset that CNN was not as properly patriotic as they thought it should have been, as when CNN reporters did not appear to be squarely on the American team in their reporting from Iraq, as well as those from abroad who still consider CNN to be just another tool of American imperalism. The latter grows out of a resentment directed at all Western news services, for lording American culture all over the world and the fact that a large part of the world can only see international events from an American perspective.

Turner acknowledges this. The Western news organizations do dominate international news. The stories they distribute are filtered through a Western orientation as to what is and is not newsworthy. Turner's answer is that, with a 24-hour news programme, there is room for more news of all types and that he intends to see that a variety of perspectives, including non-Western perspectives, are a part of CNN's coverage.

He has often talked of how he came to be more international in his own orientation. 'When I started CNN,' he has explained, 'I really didn't have any intention to go outside the United States with the service. In fact, where I got the idea that the service was of value in other countries was from Fidel Castro in Cuba'.

'When our film crews were in Cuba (in 1982), we were told by a member of Cuban television that President Castro would like to meet me, if there was an opportunity to do so. I accepted the invitation and went and spent a week in Cuba, seeing Cuban television and the various ministries and it was my first opportunity to visit a socialist country. I had all the same prejudices and preconceived notions that most people in the capitalist world had ten years ago, that when I went down there, I was going into where the enemy was, I might be kidnapped, never come home, and so forth and so on.

'In fact, the stereotypes that had been presented to me in the media were ... when I got to Havana, I thought I would see everybody walking around with their ball in their hand that was chained to their leg, with tanks on every corner and machine guns and a very unhappy group of people. And in fact, people were wearing different coloured outfits, there were no more police around than there are here in the United States and I had great conversations.

'But the whole idea is Fidel Castro was watching CNN. He had a satellite dish and he was watching it and he said it was very important for him to find out what was going on in the world'.

With *World Report*, Turner has not only given Fidel Castro a way to keep up with what is going on in the rest of the world, he has added Cuba's voice to the mix. From 1987, when *World Report* began, CRT-Cuba has aired more than 200 news stories on the CNN internationally distributed network. Wherever CNN signals come down in the world, a little bit of Cuban culture and Cuban perspective come down as well.

The *World Report* experiment

To the first *World Report* contributors conference in 1989 Turner also invited an array of international news-makers to address the meeting, including Jimmy Carter, Jesse Jackson, Oscar Arias and Javier Perez de Cuellar. Perez de Cuellar was unable to come at the last minute but sent a videotaped address. In introducing the Secretary General, Turner explained, 'Since its inception, there has been only one goal for this programme, a goal likely shared by the founders of the United Nations: to bring the people of the world closer together by letting them tell each other about themselves'.

The United Nations General Secretary spoke to the importance of *World Report* in improving international understanding. 'Ladies and gentlemen, with television's omnipresence in today's world, the accessibility of news and information to residents of all countries – though they may vary from one place to another – is unprecedented in history. Television is the town crier of the 20th century, walking through the diverse neighbourhoods of our global community. It brings us news of our neighbours from all continents and promotes worldwide understanding, the only hope for lasting peace'.

'The *CNN World Report* has been a pathfinder in this respect,' he said. 'The period during which it has been in existence has coincided with a dramatic improvement in the global environment and the media's handling of it. Many subjects that were once regarded as arcane or not newsworthy are now prominently in the public eye. Only two decades ago, there would not have been much interest from news managers in issues such as the environment, the status of women and the international debt crisis. Now they feature in front page reports and nightly news programmes. In this respect, television has helped the United Nations' own handling of important international issues by raising public awareness and changing public attitudes towards them'.

By the time the Allied Forces began their offensive to remove Iraq from Kuwait in

January 1991, the *CNN World Report* had carried some 7000 news items from 150 television news organizations representing 120 countries, including news reports prepared by Iraqi TV. Knowing the relationships which CNN had worked to establish with Third World broadcasters, it is plausible that CNN did get preferential treatment from Iraq during the invasion. And for good reason. Iraqi broadcasters had reason to be grateful to the only American news organization interested in their perspective on things. More significantly, through *World Report* and its expanding international operations, CNN had earned a reputation for treating Iraqi and other Third World television news people as professionals and as colleagues. As it happened, when Iraq suddenly emerged as 'enemy number one' in the world, Iraqi broadcast staff continued friendly relations. For CNN it was an open door to get at the news developing there.

Perhaps one reason CBS and the other US television networks were surprised and miffed that CNN already had a close working relationship with the Iraqi ministry of information was that they hadn't expected so much from a cable network, and were a little embarassed to realize the extent to which they had not done their homework in Iraq. More damaging than that perhaps was the dawning realization that along with a new political world order there was a new order in international news coverage and ABC, CBS and NBC were no longer at its centre.

CNN did not become an international contender overnight. It was in Libya in 1986 where CNN gained a reputation for being more than a bush-league news service. When then-president Ronald Reagan ordered a US bombing raid against Libya, CNN correspondent John Donovan was in Tripoli to describe the scene as it happened. Those Americans who subscribed to cable got continuous coverage from the front via CNN. In a story at the time the Champaign-Urbana *News Gazette* described this much-appreciated accomplishment in an article entitled: 'CNN's Coverage of Libya Makes Big Guys Look Bush'.[3]

Invited to the CNN conference for *World Report* contributors in May 1989 were two officials from Libya, the director of broadcasting and the director general of Libyan TV. The two never arrived because the US government wouldn't give them visas, a matter protested by CNN. Not surprisingly, Libyan relationships with CNN were and are still cordial. This is demonstrated by the LJB-Libya stories carried on *World Report*, including those of Moammar Quaddafi giving his views on the Iraqi invasion of Kuwait during the Persian Gulf crisis, and by CNN's access to Libyan sources during the UN-imposed sanctions growing out of the downing of a Pan Am airliner over Scotland.

CNN gained additional stature and more than a little respect covering the turmoil in China during and following Mikhail Gorbachev's visit there in mid-May 1989. CNN had been given the go-ahead by Chinese authorities to broadcast live reports from Beijing, including special permission to use its own fly-away satellite uplink. When the Tiananmen Square events became the better story, the effort to shut down CNN – and its only other US competitor with live coverage, CBS – became an international event. The *Chicago Tribune* reported that senior Bush administration officials were 'rivited' to the live CNN coverage in a hotel room in Kennebunkport, Maine. The *Boston Globe*'s David Hynan wrote that 'the world kept an ear cocked to CNN'.[4]

CNN's ease of entry to China and its ability to report live from China at the time of the student uprising can be tied in part to the fact that earlier in that same month Feng Xiaoming, a CCTV-China reporter and anchorman, was an invited guest in Atlanta addressing the other *CNN World Report* contributors. Prior to Tiananmen, CCTV had established a regular presence on the weekly programme, and as of 1992 has had more than 150 of its own stories aired on the *CNN World Report*.

According to Eason Jordan, the man responsible for CNN's international coverage, CNN's ability to set up a satellite up-link on the Iranian side of the Iraq-Iran border during the Persian Gulf crisis is attributable to *World Report* contacts. He notes that in attendance at the 1990 Atlanta conference of *World Report* contributors were three Iranian officials who report to the director general of Iranian TV, who happens to be the brother of Iran's president Ali Akbar Rafsanjani. As of 1992, IRIB-Iran has itself contributed 53 news stories which were aired on *World Report*.

'Trust is a factor,' says Eason Jordan. 'They saw our coverage was even-handed. That's what counts'. He notes that CNN got a quick answer from Iran on the up-link querie as a result of its personal contacts. As for China, Jordan is quick to add that after Tiannamen the English language service, which CNN regularly taped, disappeared from the air for several months and some of the *CNN World Report* contacts found themselves on the outs. There were no contributions coming from China for a time. 'The relationship is fine now'. At the time of the interview he was off to Beijing within the week and also had plans to drop by Tehran. 'Especially in those places,' he says, 'We have to work to keep the relationships alive'.

In 1980, as CNN aired its first broadcast, a United Nations Educational, Scientific, and Cultural Organization (UNESCO) committee released the results of three years' research on the state of international communication. The findings, published in a book entitled *Many Voices, One World*, focused the movement for a 'new world information order'. The committee urged the world's broadcasters to provide 'more justice, more equity, more reciprocity in information exchange, less dependence in communication flows, less downward diffusion of messages, more self-reliance and cultural identity, and more benefits for all mankind'.[5]

Leaders of the developing nations for years had been protesting the north-to-south one-way flow of international news. The complaint was that the direction of news flow was always outward from centre to periphery, from news producer to news consumer, and that coverage by reporters sent out from the more technologically developed nations was not accurately depicting life in the developing world. UNESCO helped focus these complaints and give them weight.

Ted Turner credits UNESCO for the idea of the *World Report*, which he had conceived as a kind of community channel for the whole planet. 'The good point (UNESCO) had was that the news and information travelling around this planet was controlled by the West'. He thought this was wrong. 'The *World Report* is the first chance to remedy that, where we allow everyone to speak their own words'.

The idea was to create within the context of CNN an international newscast open for wide participation, and make it a news exchange so that everybody could use everybody else's material. It would be a barter arrangement so that stations contributing would get something back. Everyone would benefit. CNN promotes the programme as 'the first global newscast and the World's largest news exchange,' and it is. The newscast is global in that the *World Report* is broadcast literally worldwide. Ninety per cent of the world's population is now within reach of at least one of the five satellites leased by CNN's 24 hour news service. The news exchange, which permits countries to submit their stories to CNN headquarters in Atlanta, is equally impressive in that *World Report* is made up of reports from all geographic regions, with TV news organizations from 130 countries having participated at one time or another.

World Report provides broadcasters the opportunity to present news of their countries, or to cover from their point of view events happening in other countries. The invitation to local television news organizations around the world to submit stories for use in the programme, and CNN's pledge to transmit the stories unedited and uncensored, responds directly to the charge that the dominant news agencies have tended to focus on the negative and that the developing world never gets to tell its own story. In exchange for news items submitted to CNN, contributors receive the rights to use as they wish any or all of the material included in the *CNN World Report*.

The global newscast

CNN details the conditions for participation in a *CNN World Report* press kit which is given to all prospective contributors. Potential contributors must meet two eligibility requirements. First, they must be an organization hosting a group of people known as professional journalists, who have the capability to prepare news reports and a way of conveying those reports to CNN headquarters in Atlanta. Second, the organization must have some way of receiving and making use of the programme in return. According to Stuart Loory, the original editor in chief of the *CNN World Report*, 'It is the philosophy of the *CNN World Report* that we be as inclusive as possible'. He says, 'We are trying to create a true marketplace of viewpoints and perspectives on the news around the world'.

The contributing news organizations pay all costs of production and delivery of their reports to CNN each week, either by satellite or by air freight. CNN assumes all costs of assembling the newscast and transmitting it via satellite to earth stations in contributing countries. Contributors are invited to down-link and rebroadcast the programme locally in its entirety, or tape the programme for later use in any way they like. For those few countries – about a dozen – who do not have down-link capabilities, CNN ships the programme by video cassette, absorbing the cost.

In the beginning, CNN was asking for a report a week but now there are so many contributors it could not possibly accommodate the influx if the 170-plus participants all suddenly decided to be regular contributors. *World Report* guidelines say that contributors may continue to receive and use the material as long as contributions occur at least once per month. In practice, the staff has been flexible about this and goes out of its way to encourage even infrequently-participating stations to use the material more. CNN reserves the right to use contributed material in its regular programming, as well as in the *World Report*, and all submissions arriving in Atlanta are archived. There are no formal contracts and no money changes hands.

World Report has set a policy of using only one story per week from each contributor, and when there is more than one contributing news organization from the same country, as is the case with Argentina, Australia, Germany, Hungary and the Philippines, the news organizations are asked to work out a voluntary submission schedule. This rule, too, has required flexibility in implementation given the political changes occuring among the republics of Yugoslavia, the Soviet Union and elsewhere. The *World Report* has held to a three-minute maximum on length of story, expecting that stories will be voiced in English (or scripts provided so the English narration can be added in Atlanta) and the staff have begged of contributors as much lead time as possible (usually two days) so they can adequately prepare stories for airing.

Although CNN promises not to change any submitted story, it reserves the right to cut the story to meet the time limit. If the contributor is unable to provide an English translation, CNN will make those arrangements. Content is solely the decision of the participating news organization. The Press Kit expresses a preference for 'hard news' with lots of good video showing what the contributor's country and life in it are like. In addition, the reports are expected to be in good taste and conform to American libel and slander laws.

While the staff has gone to great lengths not to influence the content – and especially not the perspective, on the occasion of certain worldwide events, such as the UN Earth Summit in Rio, Christmas, Ramadan, World Cup, the Non-Aligned Nations meeting, or Israeli-Palestinian talks, calls have gone out from Atlanta for local coverage on these events. In addition, a number of 'specials' or special segments around a theme, such as AIDS, hunger, the homeless, refugees and children, have been aired. Enough viewer interest has been generated by these special programmes that the staff plans to do more of this type of programming.

Initially, *World Report* aired every story that came in. The very first programme had 33 reports. CNN itself contributed a round-up of the week's news, consisting of five individual news items, as did the Soviet Union with three stories. Now CNN limits itself to a single story. No other broadcast organization from the USA, except for American Samoa, Guam, Marshall Islands and Puerto Rico, has been a participant.

Newscasts now average 30 to 40 stories each with an effort to balance representation by region. Latin America and Africa tend to be less-well-represented in terms of total number of stories offered. The number of participating news organizations from Latin America and African regions, however, is comparable to those participating from Asia and Western Europe, the regions generating the most stories.

Content studies show that the news submitted is similar to that of international news found on other services, that is, it centres around domestic and foreign politics. Since the inauguration of the programme in 1987, an increasing amount of economic news is being featured. Research also shows that, when compared to traditional Western-based news coverage of international events, *World Report* tends to focus somewhat less on military issues, crime, disasters and accidents and more on arts and culture, on ecology and the environment and on stories about science and health. There is a more equal representation of 'good news' as opposed to 'bad news'.

After two years and 105 programmes, CNN's weekly *World Report* added a daily format.

The week-end programme continued to run 3:00–5:00 p.m. EST Sundays with a repeat at mid-night airing until all stories were transmitted. The Daily Program, introduced 16 October 1989, airs Monday through Friday 3:40–3:55 p.m. EST in the second half of the CNN International Hour. The Daily *World Report* focuses on breaking news. Unlike the weekend show, the producer of the Daily solicits reports on specific topics for any given day or week. Contributors decide whether or not to report on a requested topic and the editorial content of the report is left solely up to them. Contributors' suggestions for reports on the Daily programme are encouraged, thus stories often arrive during the week which the CNN staff has the option to use.

The daily *World Report* scooped the story of Iraq's invasion of Kuwait in August 1990. The following scenario was taken from the daily journal of a CNN staff member.

Thursday, 2 August 1990 – Iraq invades Kuwait

7:00 a.m. – The producer of the CNN Daily World *World Report* is on the phone with Rana Nejem of Jordan TV and Sohair Hafez of ETV-Egypt, making arrangements for them to report on the regional situation.

10:00 a.m. – Ralph Wenge, CNN WR anchor, interviews Rana Nejem via phone on CNN air.

11:00 a.m. – Rana Nejem contacts the *World Report* to say a visual package will be ready for the 3:30 p.m. Daily *World Report*.

3:30 p.m. – Ralph Wenge spends the greater part of the daily programme interviewing Sohair Hafez on the phone from Cairo to guage the latest on Arab reaction to the invasion. The Jordan TV package is held for the following day.

No one provided television news information from the Middle East region quicker, not even other CNN programmes, than the *World Report* contributors says a CNN staff writer, 'With 180 international news organizations only a phone call away from covering the news, the global news exchange possibilities of the Daily *World Report* may present CNN with its greatest advantage over the networks'.

More recent coverage of events in Southern Africa, Eastern Europe and in the Middle East have further demonstrated the value to CNN of the arrangement. But *World Report* is proving to be more than a handier way to gather the world's news, it is the first real glimpse at the way other nations view the news.

Local news from abroad

World Report is unique in that it gives viewers a way to test the rightness and wrongness of the ideas they have. International television shows events viewers can not see with their own eyes, in places they can not go, concerning people they have never met, within cultures with which they are not familiar. Journalists are hired to translate those distant events into a familiar discourse, presenting the unfamiliar in a context that is within the viewer's experience.

Viewers are hardly ever aware that the reporter's story is an interpretation and therefore metaphorical, largely because viewers take for granted their own frames of reference. The cultural logic by which viewers organize and structure the world seems perfectly natural to them. Automatically they assume the perspective from which they view the world, whatever it is, must be the right and true one. If the images are collected by a single reporter, or there is only one service through which the news is filtered, the viewer can end up with less than a complete picture.

At the Atlanta conference hosted by CNN, Prince Sadruddin Aga Khan, coordinator of the United Nations humanitarian and economic assistance programmes for Afghanistan, urged the assembled press to try to be a part of the peace process. 'I recognize the fact that causes do not make good stories,' he said, 'and that therefore you tend to focus on the symptoms. But as far as Afghanistan is concerned, let us try to avoid stereotypes'.

Aga Khan acknowledged that in the West the Afghans had become heroes and the image of the proud Mujahadeen, the 'Muj' as they became known, was widespread. In the Soviet Union, on the other hand, they were known as 'dushman,' meaning bandits. 'Everybody knows that one man's terrorist is another man's freedom fighter. But the fact of the matter is that these were also stereotypes. The point is that first and foremost, these people were Afghans'. He praised the journalists for bringing home the horrors of war, 'Now let's try to focus on peace building'.

Because news gathering is selective, much of the world's news is missed. Unless people make a special effort to find out by other means, it is unlikely those who get their news by television will have any idea what is going on in three-quarters of the countries of the world at any given time. Vietnam, a country that made the news almost every night for a decade, has all but disappeared from American airwaves except in the contributions which Vietman TV itself regularly makes to *World Report*. Those who watch *World Report* on CNN will have learned that Vietnam is anxious to heal the wounds that distance it from the West. Perhaps only on CNN will viewers have seen reports on the Vietnamese boat people repatriated from Hong Kong and the establishing of legal means for boat people to immigrate, on Vietnam's efforts to co-operate in locating American MIAs and on addressing the problem of the Amerasian children of US GIs, now outcasts in Vietnamese society.

To take another example, via TV3-Catalunya *World Report* viewers will have witnessed residents of the Spanish town of Vandellos taking to the streets in celebration of the closing of one of the country's ten nuclear power stations, they will have seen that relations between Spain and Cuba have plunged to an all-time low, and that a woman in Spain has been given the legal right to choose the sex of her child.

And, among the reports aired from TV Manchete-Brazil have been the usual stories on the Carnival celebrations in Rio. But in other reports TV Manchete has examined the problems of the more than seven million street children in Brazil, has shown the threats to Brazil's Amazon rainforest and discussed the Brazilian economy, which is crippled by drastic inflation. Such stories are of interest not just because they show what news is being missed by established news sources in distant places like Vietnam, Spain and Brazil but because they bring out differences in reporting which shape and colour perception.

There is no one answer to the question, 'what is *World Report* news?,' for it is whatever events or experiences or perspectives local broadcast news organizations choose to share by means of the CNN channel. In substance, it is protest, it is festival, advertisement, manifesto, tragedy and novelty. In topical categories it is not unlike the news seen on television elsewhere. Only, in this instance, there is a much richer cultural mix and not one but a hundred or more different points of view.

Some countries are regular contributors, rarely missing the opportunity, but most report only sporadically. The appearance of their news is therefore noteworthy, for it marks a decision to say something. Since *World Report* stories originate from and are attributed to countries, the information being conveyed goes well beyond that pertaining to a specific event. Inevitably, these stories not only tell what is happening (or what, out of all that is happening, is considered worth telling), they are statements about how different people in different places perceive and structure reality, or how they would like others to see what they see.

As a contributor to *CNN World Report*, for example, YLE-Finland says its selects mostly hard-news topics 'which could interest people in more than two or three countries and which represent Finnish television news reporting style adapted in English'. Kristian Aberg, news coordinator at OY Yleisradio, explains 'We also try to select every now and then some cultural or lifestyle stories that might have something to offer to a wider audience than our own'.

Is the news item produced in Finland and shown on Finnish television the same story when dubbed and translated and rebroadcast in the USA? Inevitably it becomes something of a different story. Even if there is no change in content, it has changed in terms of who the story is aimed at. Who the audience is changes the purpose, value and meaning of the story. Neither the language, with all its power, nor the familiar stage on which the news is read is in any way the same. The Colombian story about the drug lords of Medellin is still about Medellin drug lords but on CNN it now shares a space not with other Colombian news but with news items from Ecuador, Brazil, Yugoslavia and China. The point of the story, its relevance to the intended audience, picks up entirely new meanings. As international news, it becomes the country of Colombia speaking about itself.

Such a diversity of sources and cultural accents is ideal for comparing the ways different societies choose to present their news, for noting differences in reporting style, treatment, emphasis and priority, and for observing the contrast between news aimed at an international audience and news intended for those back home. To us, the way of the West seems so naturally to be the way of doing broadcast journalism, but as observed on *World Report*, other formats do exist, other news priorities are given attention.

Such a service provides a way of seeing how the once voiceless world community can begin to use the language of television to speak of itself, to tell the world what is important from its point of view. *CNN World Report* gives the first chance some nations of the world have ever had to be listened to outside their own borders.

References

1. Craig Leddy, 'CNN Grabs Spotlight in Live TV War,' *Electronic Media*, January 21, 1991.
2. *Electronic Media*, May 6, 1991.

3. John Bowman, 'CNN's Coverage of Libya Makes Big Guys Look Bush, *Champaign-Urbana News Gazette*, April 20, 1986.

5. David Hynan, 'CNN in China: A Triumph,' *Boston Globe* (in CNN Newsbrief, September, 1989.)

6. Sean MacBride, *Many Voices, One World*, Paris: UNESCO, 1980.

Chapter 2   NEW ORDER JOURNALISM

'It's not the same audience that watches football on Sunday afternoons'.
Ralph Wenge, CNN World Report anchor

Among the hundreds of letters arriving at CNN every day was a note from a high school biology teacher from Los Angeles. 'Your two-hour special report on World Population is the most important and well-done special report I have ever seen on television!,' his letter said. Writing in longhand, his enthusiasm for the *World Report* programme could be read from his script as well as in what he had to say. 'You have done humanity a great service by producing and broadcasting this special. Your presentation convincingly demonstrates the great suffering mankind can be spared if we can get the population explosion under control. I hope you will air it again and make it available to educators. Thank you'.

The *CNN World Report* is not the only programme on the air addressing such issues as population explosion. It is the only place where viewers can regularly catch the perspectives of the world's most affected nations, rich or poor, on issues of common concern. Or, hear issues raised that may not yet have reached the level of importance to be classified as 'international news'. What is noteworthy about *World Report* is that so many more topics are put on the agenda and audiences find out there can be so many more ways of viewing the same subject. This difference relates to World Report's operating philosophy, the open-ended rules of the exchange, and the unique division of responsibility between the CNN staff and the programme's many contributors.

Philosophy

The operating philosophy, the body of ideas that makes the service what it is, is a key to understanding what *World Report* is all about. Unlike any other news programme you can think of, *World Report* exists to present as many international viewpoints as possible, uncensored and without editorial comment. It proceeds on the rather startling assumption that all viewpoints are valid components of reality, whether they are objective or not. CNN's approach to *World Report* has been to make no judgement about right and wrong versions of the news, but to focus on identifying as many different perspectives as can be found, the more views expressed on a given issue the better. Editorial judgements about whether the information is relevant or timely or presented in a balanced way are deferred to the viewer. For those who know something about the way news organizations operate, this is not the typical model.

Stuart Loory, CNN vice president who was the founding producer of *CNN World Report*, envisioned the programme as a place where news reports of different perspectives could compete for attention, a place where professional journalists from any of the world's television organizations could post reports and be assured that their material would appear undiluted and undistorted in any way. This alone makes *World Report* distinctive. For an internationally-distributed news service to offer a virtually guaranteed slot to local broadcasters to report the news as they think it should be reported, prior to *CNN World Report*, was basically an unthinkable idea.

'After starting CNN itself,' Ted Turner told a radio-television news directors association meeting in Kansas City, 'I think the best thing we've done is *World Report*. Basically it's just giving people in the smaller countries, and countries over the world, a chance to be heard from'.

'It's just really amazing,' he said. 'As an American, I always thought of the world as 'President Reagan talked to Margaret Thatcher' or 'President Bush talks to Gorbachev' but on *World Report* you'll see the president of an African country meeting with another African leader. And that never makes the news here'.[1]

In *World Report*, Turner says, CNN has made a commitment to presenting news from the perspectives of professional journalists throughout the world. This will better enable 'the world's television viewers to explore all lands'.

Turner told a group of *World Report* contributors of his reaction when Carl Sagan, the space scientist, was describing the huge receiving antennas pointed into outerspace which monitor radio frequencies with the intent of listening for messages from life beyond earth. 'I was saying to myself, 'My God. We didn't have a system to even find out what was going on from the various nations of the world until the *World Report* came around'. The audience appreciated his remarks and gave him a hearty applause when he told them, 'I guarantee if you've watched the *World Report* like I do – the wealth of information there – it's like going to other planets ... it's like coming from a different world'.

Stuart Loory says the idea for *World Report* took shape during a trip Ted Turner made to India. Upon return to Atlanta Turner's ears were ringing with complaints from Third World leaders about how nothing significant in their countries was ever considered news. TV people in the developing countries were angry that they couldn't get a story told in the Western media and that 'American journalism only covered tragedies – Bhopal, revolution, mayhem – and then we go away,' according to Loory. 'Ted got back from India and said let's allow an international spectrum of journalists to produce stories, and we'll put them on the air'.

Turner told *World Report* contributors, 'I read the UNESCO reports and various international magazines about how there was a great deal of discomfort, particularly in the smaller countries and the less-wealthy countries, that all the flow of news around the world was controlled by the large countries, to a great degree by the great powers of the West. The only time that India was ever mentioned in the news was when there was a war or a rebellion or a Bhopal. And it's not right,' he said. 'That was where I came up with the idea that in the *World Report* we would have a regular place where everybody in the world could be heard, where, for the first time, everybody in the world has the opportunity to speak to everybody else on a regular basis'.

Three years after the inauguration of world Report on CNN, Turner invited a volunteer group called the Friendship Force to meet with him over lunch in his office in Atlanta. The Friendship Force had helped find home-stay accommodations in Atlanta for international journalists participating in CNN's special training programme for *World Report* contributors. He wanted to show his appreciation. Someone in the group put a friedly challenge to Turner. 'You wouldn't use news from an enemy?' Turner said he hadn't thought about that until *World Report* came along but decided it was worth a try. 'If you open your heart to others, they will open their heart to you,' he said.

'Out of ignorance grows fear and out of fear grows protection – getting a bigger gun. The way of breaking that is putting people in contact. The worst thing you can do,' he said, 'you take away a man's voice'.

TV Guide published a commentary by Gene Keys in which he described *World Report* as a come-as-you-are forum for the world community's many different TV news organizations, regardless of country or ideology or degree of media polish. 'It's one of those rare examples of TV's power to do something enormously good – in this case provide a global vista unhomogenized by New York or Toronto, and from locals other than Washington or Moscow'.[15]

Turner admits to being a do-gooder. 'Before CNN I was a good person but I wasn't socially motivated,' he says. 'When I started CNN I said I have to be more informed. I learned (when I went to Cuba) that most of what I thought before was wrong. I believed the Soviets were our sworn enemies and that we were all doomed'.

The Goodwill Games were in direct response to Turner's social activism, as was the weekly environmental programme Future Watch on CNN. CNN Newsroom, a daily programme of news for the public schools which is offered without commercial advertisements, and the animated series for children, Captain Planet, which carries only environmentally correct ads, are programmes consistent with the socially-relevant television programming Turner thinks important in our time. He has signed long-term production agreements with the Audubon Society and the Cousteau Society and produced movies and documentaries and advertising campaigns designed, as his staff says, 'to change the course of the planet'.

'It's one world,' says Turner. 'We are going to make it together or not make it at all'.

'CNN is a commercial operation,' says a CNN staff member, 'but CNN is probably the only news organization in the USA that hasn't placed any importance on numbers'. The idea is, having a significant audience is important in the long run but the way to attract viewers to news is not to poll their preferences. Prior to the Persian Gulf crisis, when CNN earned audience ratings which pushed viewership to levels competitive with the commercial broadcast networks, almost no audience research was done at CNN and what was done was not circulated to the staff. According to Lynn Gutstadt, director of research for CNN and CNN Headline News, Ted Turner did not want his news people to be concerned about who was watching. He told them, 'Just do news the way it should be done. Let me worry about our competitive position'.

The traditional approach of commercial broadcasters is to survey for audience preferences and create programmes based on what the studies say audiences are interested in. To some extent news has been held aloof from this practice, but news inevitably becomes part and parcel of programming designed to draw viewers, improve ratings and sell advertisements. In effect, the commercial media, in trying to be sensitive to their audiences, have come to rely on the public to set their programming agendas. Certainly Turner runs a for-profit operation too, but there is a slightly different business strategy to be noted.

Speaking to the radio and television news directors at the RTND convention in Kansas City, Turner asked, 'What is news? You know what news is? News is what you news directors interpret it as. News is what we at CNN interpret it as. The people of this country see the news that we think they oughta see. And quite frankly, a lot of that decision is geared to what's gonna keep them interested, keep them at your station'.[2]

The amount of air time devoted by CNN to the Clarence Thomas US Supreme Court confirmation hearings and to the trial of William Kennedy Smith, are examples. CNN drew record audiences in its coverage of these two events. At the same time it put before the public as never before issues of date rape and sexual harassment in the workplace.

No commercial broadcaster can afford to ignore audience interests and tastes. Yet, there is apparently room in the market for broadcasters who choose to lead their audience, to take a hand in shaping public perception as to the issues. This willingness to take such risks is consistent with Turner business practice, as well as his social activism, and shows up in the *World Report* experiment, a programme which is intended to focus public attention and confer status on issues of global concern. This is not the power to control, or even the power to bring about change, but to set the agenda.

When the media play up an issue or cover an event, the public eventually comes to regard that issue or event as significant. Research confirms this to be true. Likewise, when the media do not pay attention to persons, places and occasions, those cannot be long viewed as important. To this extent, by their choice of news, the media determines the issues the public thinks about.[3]

'TV has become a news maker as much as a news reporter. There is no news where there is no camera today,' Prince Sadruddin Aga Khan, United Nations humanitarian and economic assistance coordinator, told the assembled *World Report* contributors at one of the CNN-hosted conferences. 'When they decided to clamp down on news in South Africa or Israel, some people believed that there was nothing wrong in those parts of the world. That somehow the struggle for civil rights, human rights, receded in the southern part of Africa. And some people probably believed that the Intefada somehow has gone out of steam in the Middle East'. China, he said, has been facing momentous upheavals. 'We never hear about it'.

What is heard on *World Report* that would have gone unnoticed by the world's TV audiences? Namibia's explanations why it authorized the extermination of 20,000 seals in the waters off its coast, reported by the Namibian Broadcasting, and the dismay and outrage in Thailand, where 90 per cent of the population is Buddhist, that six Buddhist monks could be murdered in the United States, reported by Army TV Channel 5-Thailand, are the kind of stories that would have gone unreported. The fact that Switzerland is a haven for gun smugglers as a result of a powerful pro-gun lobby which assures liberal gun laws and that Zimbabwe has the potential to be a coal-exporting nation but lacks the transportation to bring the coal to the world market, are perhaps not momentus stories but, from the perspective of the international viewer, they are at least as important as the Clarence Thomas hearings and the William Kennedy Smith trial.

With 35 to 40 of these type stories offered each week, *World Report* has created its own need to exist, carving out its own market and producing a demand where there was no obvious audience. When *World Report* first aired, say the *World Report* staff, there was no assurance that a good cross-section of the world's broadcasters would be able to participate, even if they wanted to, or that the viewing public would accept and use the programme or that advertisers would support it. Now that world broadcasters do regularly contribute, with many taking stories in exchange for local use, and CNN showing audience ratings for *World Report* at least equal to its 24-hour viewership, it has apparently found the niche that makes it a viable operation.

The notion that out of free and open communciations will come public debate and out of public debate will emerge truth, and the idea that the press has a responsibility to serve and advance society, is a well-established tradition in Western journalism. *World Report* appears to be an extension of the 'socially responsible press' philosophy, which has as its basis the concept that in a global society the public is best served through the airing of multiple points of view, even unpopular positions, and that the public can be better informed when, among the reporting and interpretation and analysis of world events, there are also given views which do not necessarily tell the public what it wants to hear.

With *World Report*, CNN takes on a more overt kind of socially responsible commercialism. By inviting in the world's broadcasters and by putting its own resources into the timely distribution of news to all points on the globe, more news is available. With more news available from so many different points of view, news consumption increases. The news market is broadened and deepened. By using an inclusive and co-operative approach to getting out the news, rather than the more typical exclusive-competitive approach, the number of players and the number of perspectives is greatly enhanced. Thus, if Ted Turner has his way, international conflict will be less and international understanding will be greater. Out of that, Turner hopes to have created a market for a product that will pay its bills and allow his company to grow.

There are big 'ifs' in this approach, but unless there is a social responsibility principle operating among the world's broadcasters, there is no way two-thirds of the countries of the world will be heard from. Neither authoritarian or libertarian approaches will serve the need. Authoritarians believe the state is in the best position to decide what is best for their constituent publics to read and see and hear, which leads most often to only one view of world events being presented. On the other hand, libertarians assume that in a free marketplace of ideas all viewpoints that have worth will get aired, a principle which ignores the fact that due to inequitable access to resources, the only news distributed around the world will be what is collected by those with the economic backing to do so.

Any month will do, but to take February 1990 as illustration, it is easy to see how *World Report* fills a void. In the first week of the month, Yugoslavia's JRT-TV Belgrade and JRT-TV Ljubljana led the programme with separate reports on the situation in Kosovo – one from the Serbian perspective, the other from the Slovenian. TRT-Turkey and ERT-Greece in the same programme provided different perspectives on recent clashes between Moslems and Christians in Western Thrace. The increased immigration of Soviet Jews to the West Bank was covered by correspondents from JTV-Jordan, IBA-Israel and ETV-Egypt.

In the following week, ICRT-Cuba led with a report voicing concerns that Third World needs would be overlooked, now that developed countries were focusing their attention on the political and economic changes taking place in Eastern Europe. In the same newscast, SABC-South Africa, SWABC-Namibia and Globalvision all followed Mandela's first days of freedom, each from its own perspective. The issue of German unification was examined not only by Deutsche Welle-West Germany but also by TVP-Poland and by Global TV-Canada.

The CNN Daily *World Report*, in the third week, carried reactions on the up-coming Nicaraguan Presidential elections from ICRT-Cuba and Canal 7-Costa Rica, as well as SSTV-Nicaragua.

With these 'perspectives on the news,' the question of bias is less of a red flag when taken in the context of what *World Report* is all about. With *World Report*, the staff say, it is understood that a point of view is possible and probably inevitable in any good reporting and there is nothing wrong with a story with an argument. Not every story, within itself, has to be balanced so long as the viewer also has access to arguments from the other side.

What *World Report* does is give viewers the means to be more critical, recognizing that what they see on television is collected from an assortment of political and other perspectives. Allowing viewers to make up their own minds, according to *World Report* staffers, is just what the world public wants the freedom to do. They say viewers want to hear what the Russians, the Cubans, the Nicaraguans, the South Africans think and they don't mind hearing it directly from them.

In response to questions about the 'objectivity' of the news appearing on *CNN World Report* and its succeptibility to bias, given its open format, former associate producer Brooke McDonald told a journalist from a cable magazine, 'The idea is that we've created a forum or a marketplace for ideas. And what is propaganda to one person is valid news to another, depending upon your point of view. It's not propaganda if you have several points of view expressed'.[4]

'What I've been able to realize is how differently everybody sees things,' she says. 'Seeing events from other countries from the point of view of the people who live there gives you a very different feeling for life in that country'. She notes that *World Report* is a step in the direction of moving away from the crisis journalism that is so apparent on US news.

On *CNN World Report*, says McDonald, 'We're able to see both sides of life – the ordinary things that are the brighter parts of life in a country as well as the crises'. Good things also happen in Colombia, she noted, but all we ever hear about Colombia in the US news is the violence. On *World Report*, the things that the country is most proud of will be shown as well, 'like a doctor who's working on a cure for malaria, and an international film festival they've just had'.

All news is selective, the argument goes. Western reporters select their news for Western audiences from a Western point of view. In emphasizing some things, they must leave other things out. It is the nature of reporting. International reporters are trained to find the story in unfamiliar, often chaotic, situations, to give their reports an attention-getting angle based on a judgement about what their desk editors will and will not like and what will go over with the home audience. Such decisions involve predispositions, prior instructions and assumptions abut audiences. And it is a given that covering the story quickly, simply and in a language the home audience can understand leads to over-simplification and stereotyping.

'To say that we do not have a point of view is dishonest,' Jesse Jackson told the *World Report* contributors at a CNN conference. 'We ought to have a point of view, and put our diverse points of view in the marketplace and test them, and not be so arrogant as to assume that our point of view is the only point of view,' he said, '... somewhere we'll find a creative synthesis and make common ground'.

'We live in a one world house, a one world community,' Jackson told conferees. 'Most people in the world are yellow or brown or black, non-christian, poor, female, young and don't speak English. So there can be no world news tonight that does not speak of the yellow, the brown, the black, the poor, the female, the young and the disinherited'.

He told *World Report* contributors he hoped 'when you journalists leave this place, that you'll stop thinking about foreign policy. The world is too small for us to be foreigners'. He said that foreign policy should be changed to an international neighbour policy.

At the same conference, Bjorn Hansen, NRK-Norway, asked Brooke McDonald if *World Report* could use an international report from NRK-Norway on another country, even if the report might conflict with the stories produced by people from that country. He explained that his news organization maintains 10 or 11 correspondents around the world. He gave the example of a story from the Soviet Union, where NRK-Norway had a correspondent who had very good contacts with dissidents. He asked, 'What if our report conflicts with the views of the people reporting for Soviet television for you'.

McDonald's answer was, 'We love them. That's when we are doing our job best. That's when the *World Report* is at its very best. When we see the same issue from several points of view. So we will welcome them. Send them to us, please'.

As to one country reporting on another, such as Norway reporting on the USSR or Globalvision reporting on South Africa, McDonald's boss, Stuart Loory, had the same kind of response. 'We have had objections to that kind of reporting and we have had to say that we ask our contributors to feed us what they feel is important news of the moment, either from their country, or from any other country about the world, or from any region. And that is so that we continue to get all different points of view on the story'. From the point of view of *CNN World Report*, he said, the idea is to get to each viewer multiple perspectives, so that each can better understand that issues can have more than one side.

CNN anchor and host of the week-end *World Report*, Ralph Wenge, gave encouragement to contributors and explained why it is so important to have the different perspectives. 'If it were possible to get all the people in the world together under one big roof, wouldn't that be a wonderful thing? But we can't do that, can we? So we have to do it for them, we have to talk not to them but with them, to make them understand what is going on in the world ... . That is why your reports, your perspectives are so very, very important to us and to our viewers'.

'I think a lot of us in the media think people still just want local and national news. But it's a smaller world. The idea that viewers only care what's going on within the borders of the United States is no longer true'.

Wenge read from a letter from a Lebanese family now living in the USA. 'This note is to thank you for your recent report and special on Lebanon. At last someone is concerned about us Lebanese. Thank you again. We hope it's not going to be your last report on us. We must all support and we have to have your support. The government seems to be untouched about our problem. You seem to be doing better for us'.

A correspondent from Haiti told the conference that *CNN World Report* needs to be seen more in the Third World. Why? There are fewer channels to choose from. There are often no alternative or conflicting points of view. 'Haiti doesn't know what is happening with its neighbours. Cuba for example. Or the Dominican Republic. Without some shared media experience Haitians will never understand the Dominicans, although they share the same island'.

He also affirmed, 'You can't put *good* Haitian news on the air in America. But with *CNN World Report* they will take it'.

Eduard Sagaleyev, VREMYA editor, explained why TSS, the state television network of the USSR, was a regular contributor to CNN's *World Report* and used its stories in it's own newscasts. The service was a necessary first step, he said, in helping to eliminate erroneous ideas that people have about each other. 'For many years, not only did we in our country create specific stereotypes about the lives of people in capitalist countries, but in the West too, stereotypes were created of the Soviet people'. It was his view that, 'Until we eliminate the stereotypes, we journalists cannot consider that we have in fact fulfilled our duty'.

He is now convinced, he said, that 'truth is a sign of strength and if we ourselves speak the truth, then we should in no way be afraid of information from abroad, from outside'. He noted that for many years the people of the USSR simply associated information originating from the government with lies. 'Now people want to think for themselves, they want to determine for themselves what their attitude is toward one or another event in the world. But you can't have pure information. The point probably is that of not imposing our point of view, but proposing it so that the TV viewer will simply know of the existence of a number of other points of view and then he can choose the one which he feels is most appropriate to him'.

Rules

World Report is also unique in the way it works. Everything is done by a kind of gentleman's agreement. In exchange for news items, Turner Broadcasting pledges to run all stories exactly as offered. The basic guidelines are that contributions must be voiced in English, they must be three minutes or less in length and within the bounds of law and good taste. The rules are not much more than that.

Broadcast news organizations contributing stories are free to use all or some or none of the final news package which CNN assembles as *World Report*. This news exchange is a barter arrangement, not a cash transaction. As for copyright, it is the responsibility of contributors to certify that they have cleared the rights to all material submitted, which includes the audio as well as the pictures. Contributors thus grant to CNN and all other members of the exchange legal access to their work, so that everybody ends up with rights to everything that goes out on the programme. Bookkeeping and legal hassles are kept to a minimum.

There are guidelines as to who is eligible to participate, though as of 1992 these are loosely applied and still seem to be in a process of definition. When the programme went on the air in October 1987, CNN let it be known that any broadcast organization was free to contribute news. There was no way for the Turner people to know in advance exactly who would come forward, or what criteria if any needed to be established. Wishing to be as open as possible, and not an exclusive club, there was no thought to setting rigid conditions for joining.

But CNN did soon have to address the issue. Cyprus was not the first to raise the question of eligibility limits but Cyprus brought the question to the foreground. When a second contributor from Cyprus, Bayrak Television, began submitting news to *World Report*, CYBC-Cyprus protested and asked CNN for a definition of a 'broadcasting organization'.

'There is no Turkish Cyprus,' declared Themis Themistocleous, 'as there is no Greek Cyprus. There is no North, as there is no South. No Artic Cyprus, as there is no Antartic Cyprus. There is one state, one country, the Republic of Cyprus, part of which is under foreign occupation. This position is confirmed by the United Nations, the Non-Aligned Movement, the Commonwealth, the European Community, the Council of Europe and the Community of Nations, with the exception of one country, Turkey, which is the occupation power'.

'(We appreciate that CNN) is free to invite anyone,' said the CYBC-Cyprus broadcaster. 'We only wanted to point out that CNN is, regrettably, I believe, being taken advantage of in this case by an illegal regime to promote itself via its station'.

In reply, Stuart Loory sought to explain CNN's position, 'It is the philosophy of the *CNN World Report* that we be as inclusive as possible, rather than exclusive. That means that we are trying to create a true marketplace of viewpoints and perspectives on the news around the world'. He went on to say that CNN was not in the business of recognizing or not recognizing political jurisdictions. In the case of Cyprus, CNN acknowledged that the Turkish Republic of Northern Cyprus is recognized by only one other country in the world and that is Turkey.

'We also understand that Bayrak Television is an organization that meets two criteria that we have for inclusion in the *CNN World Report*. One is that it has a group of people who are known as professional journalists, who are preparing news reports and in some way disseminating those reports. The other criterion is that it has some way of taking the *CNN World Report* in return (for further dissemination)'.

Loory went on to say, 'Yours is not the only situation in which we have had problems. And I ask you, as you make that protest and as we recognize that protest, to also recognize that there are many other situations around the world where something like this could come up'. He asked CYBC-Cyprus to think about what its feelings would be if CNN were to take the kind of stand that they were asking for in other areas of the world.

'For example, we have material from South African Broadcasting Corporation. That is the recognized single, sole, legitimate broadcaster in South Africa. We also take material (as you know) from an organization called South Africa Now/Globalvision, which is headquartered in New York City. South Africa Now/Globalvision meets the kind of criteria that we are talking about. It serves to give the audience of the *CNN World Report* an alternative point of view. Suppose we were to exclude South Africa Now?'

'I have had problems, as a matter of fact, with some organizations that have not joined the *CNN World Report* because they do not want to take part in a programme that recognizes South African Broadcasting Corporation as a legitimate, news gathering, news disseminating organization. I have had to say to those organizations 'I am sorry, but I cannot be exclusive to accommodate you'.'

Loory further notes that questions have come up about a correspondent from one country going into another country to report the news, for example in a country where CNN has an arrangement with the state broadcaster. 'We have had objections to that kind of reporting and we have had to say that we ask our contributors to feed us what they feel is the important news of the moment, either from their country, or from any other country around the world, or from any region. And that is so that we continue to get all different points of view on the story'.

On another occasion, Loory was asked whether *World Report* would accept news contributions from free-lancers. 'No, we don't accept packages from independent contributors on a freelance basis. We deal with TV news organizations, for the most part broadcast news organizations. We don't deal with individual journalists or people. My arrangement, with some exceptions, is with organizations. If there are more than one broadcaster in a country, for example in Sweden there is SV1 and SV2, we'll deal with both of them, or as many as there are'.

One of the rules that was later added had to do with running more than one piece from the same country. After almost a year in which the German cablecaster, Eureka, was the only contributor, Tele-Faz, ZDF and Deutsch Welle all began sending in stories from West Germany. CNN asked the staff of those organizations to consult with each other and agree on a rotation schedule from their country. Yugoslavia was asked to do the same. In both cases, the guidelines required flexibility, since West and East Germany, each regular contributors, were in the process of re-uniting while the republics of Yugoslavia were in the process of splitting apart.

In the opening weeks of *World Report*, contributors were submitting and *World Report* was airing more than one news item per show from the same news organization. The USSR, an early contributor, was using its three minutes to get in several stories. CNN, the only US contributor to the newscast, was doing the same. This soon changed. Policies were adopted which permitted stations, for convenience or reasons of cost, to send along more than one story each week, but contributors were advised only one story would be aired. CNN thereafter carried no more than one of its own stories on the *World Report* each week and followed the same principle in airing the contributions of others. (It should be pointed out, however, that CNN regular news surrounds *World Report* and there have been instances in which CNN has interrupted or even pre-empted the programme when it has felt more pressing news – such as the US trial of former Panamanian President Manuel Noriega – should be aired. In recent years, on-the-hour news up-dates from the CNN network have been added to all CNN special features, including *World Report*.)

The daily *World Report* programme, which fits into the afternoon International Hour, does not operate under the same guidelines as the weekend *World Report*. The Daily Program is limited to a 12 to 15 minute time block – carefully set off from CNN's own material – focusing on breaking news. Unlike the weekly programme, specific news stories are requested of *World Report* contributors or selected from among the pieces that have already arrived for the weekend show. Weekend or daily *World Report* material can be repeated numerous times on CNN, on Headline News or used on one of the special programmes such as Future Watch or Health Week or Science and Technology Today.

Loory describes the weekly *World Report* as a cooperative, a friendly working agreement among professional journalists. The rest of CNN is a commercial operation. Fees are paid for news CNN picks up and uses on its network and fees are assessed based on the amount of CNN material other news organizations use. *CNN World Report* is a different model, with CNN serving as the hub of an on-going international news barter.

'I think the secret to the *CNN World Report* success is that we have kept everything very simple,' Loory said. 'So simple that I don't even have written contracts with any of our contributors. Everything is done on a handshake between journalists. It keeps the lawyers, and the business people, and everybody else out of it. The other thing is that we are not rigid. We do not tie ourselves to strict forms or formalities that prohibit us from doing things that we know should be done to increase the level of the flow of international information'.

One of CNN's viewers, writing from Bellingham, Washington, picked up on this point.

> 'Dear Moving Force: Your Sunday night programme of news and other information from elsewhere places on the planet we all live on is to the electronic media what the steam engine was to the machine age. How refreshing it is to accumulate bits and pieces of information directly from the source – other than after the information has been sifted through by salaried people who have been programmed to think that they know what I should be allowed to know and not know ... P.S. please do not allow any business professionals or FCC bureaucrats to get control of this segment of your programming'.

Staffing

Success of the *CNN World Report* depends on an unusual combination of home and field staff, some of whom are on CNN's payroll but more who are not. Both types are, in their own way, unique to international news gathering and are something of a bold – and risky – personnel venture for CNN.

World Report's in-house staff is a small 'TV Peace Corps' within the Turner organization made up of idealistic young people who work long hours for almost no pay because they believe in CNN and the cause which *World Report* represents. The reporters and producers in the field, those who work for the approximately 185 broadcast organizations in 130 countries who generate the news and deliver it to Atlanta in time for the weekly newscast, are a mixture of everything from BBC-style professionals, to those who are political appointees learning the news business as they go, to the one-person reporter who does his/her own writing, camera and editing work, often racing to the airport just in time to get the cassette on the last plane heading for the USA.

In 1991, the designated staff of *World Report* consisted of thirteen women and four men, two of whom were African-Americans, one of Hispanic heritage and three internationals (Ted Turner has outlawed the word 'foreign' within his organization). Religious affiliations were mainly Judeo-Christian. With one exception, all staff people were college graduates with approximately half holding graduate degrees. Many held degrees in fields other than journalism or communications. Almost all spoke second, and sometimes third or fourth, languages. As is true of CNN as a whole, most of the staff were in the early stages of their careers.[5]

In its new role as international newscaster, CNN has articulated the goal of presenting comprehensive global news coverage to an increasingly international audience. CNN President Thomas Johnson, who was recruited by Turner in 1990 from the Los Angeles Times, has re-articulated the goal of the *World Report* as one of encouraging individual nations to find the news, cover it and broadcast it to the world via CNN. *World Report* staff seem drawn to this mission. Several of the staff people interviewed identified the ideology of *World Report* – of providing a forum for international perspectives – as being part of what attracted them to their positions. *World Report* is a cause they believe in.

These attitudes are apparently admired and emulated by *World Report* contributors. Many of the agencies participating in *World Report* do so at considerable effort, producing and delivering stories with no hope of monetary compensation. Since most *World Report* submissions are news stories prepared especially for airing on CNN and since the originating station has the responsibility for air freight and satellite feeds to Atlanta, there are extra costs. In individual cases, reporters have been known to work on these stories beyond their assigned duties, often paying expenses out of their own pockets, and sometimes taking personal and political risks to be involved with the programme.

Octavia Nasr, LBC-Lebanon news anchor, spoke to the question of risk at a 1990 contributor conference in Atlanta. 'Is journalism dangerous in Lebanon? I'll answer by saying that sailing twelve hours from Lebanon to Cyprus, then flying fifteen hours to Atlanta to attend this conference was easier for me than driving twenty minutes to my home in Lebanon. That's how much life in general and the life of a journalist in particular is dangerous in a country like Lebanon'.

'Since 13 March 1990, I have been staying at my station, sleeping in my office on a mattress on the floor. You may be asking 'Why?' And I'll tell you that the sin I have committed is that I happen to be living in an area that is at war with the area in which I work. Worse than that, the station in which I work happens to be loyal to the Lebanese Forces Militia – this is the major Christian militia in Lebanon – at war with General Aoun, former commander of the army, occupying the presidential palace and refusing to surrender to the legitimate government'.

'Worst of all is that I am against Aoun and I refused to interview him after an incident that took place at the presidential palace. Due to all this, it was better for me to stay where I was, for if I go home my life is in danger. And this danger ranges from kidnapping, to torture, to imprisonment, or simply death'.

Nasr went on to say there is no freedom of speech or freedom of expression in Lebanon due to the prevailing anarchy. 'Journalists are labeled no matter how objective they are. In one way or the other, you feel yourself pushed to take a stand'. She noted, 'Before this last war, I was counted among the most ojective reporters in Lebanon. When the war between the Lebanese Forces and General Aoun broke out, I had to choose between two things: either stay at home doing nothing, supporting oppression and misbehavior of youngsters carrying arms and guns, or go to work, be active and perform my duties as a journalist. Of course, I chose to go to work'. (Octavia Nasr now works for CNN as a producer in the *World Report* office in Atlanta.)

Haameed Naweed, who came to the Atlanta conference representing the Afghan Media Resource Center, a rebel media organization operating out of Pakistan, made it clear that the stories they are working hard to contribute 'are not just a collection of curiosities'. He emphasized, 'People are risking their lives to tell a story'.

When CNN's Ralph Wenge asked Naweed to be interviewed on the daily *World Report*, he declined, explaining that his family is in Pakistan and he feared for their safety. Ironically, after Naweed returned to Pakistan, Center officials dismissed him for off-hand remarks he had made at the conference critical of his own organization, comments which were picked up and printed by a fellow journalist.

Mweli Mzizi, anchor of the anti-apartheid South Africa Now programme which has aired more than 100 news items on the *CNN World Report*, explained that his programme had been publicly denounced by the South African Minister of Defense and that he personally had been cast by pro-government newspapers within South Africa as being a member of the outlawed African National Congress. It caused him concern for his life. 'So I'd like to know if there's any kind of protection journalists can offer?'

In response, *World Report* senior producer Henry Schuster spoke to all contributors. 'We appreciate,' he said, 'that many of you make incredible sacrifices for the reports that you make, whether they be personal – the hours that you spend – or whether they be political. We want you to know that we appreciate those sacrifices and we are aware of them and we hope that everyone else is aware of them'. Schuster's only reassurance was the hope that 'the higher the profile that you do have, the more protection that does afford you. If you are seen worldwide on *CNN World Report* that does give you some sort of protection'.

All sacrifices are not so dramatic, but they are sacrifices nontheless. Goldbright Young, foreign news chief for TTV-Taiwan, has also been responsible for more than 100 news items from his country during the four years the programme has been on the air. He has a very small crew, he says, 'and the three of us can only devote a very small part of our time and energy to this special assignment, so small the quality of our contribution is hardly being guaranteed'.

In Taiwan, he explained, there is no English TV news programme. 'In view of this, my effort to join the family of *CNN World Report* contributors is meant for a long term purpose: that someday it will help TTV put up its first English TV news programme in Taiwan. However, much to my disappointment, my company doesn't seem to have attached due importance to this undertaking. What is really upsetting is that we hardly get any encouragement and assistance from the company, be it financial or human resources. This is really discouraging. If it were not for our personal commitment and our seriousness about the *CNN World Report* contributions, I would say our contributions must have come to a stop a long time ago'.

Even though ETV-Ethiopia's equipment was in disrepair with little chance for improvement, the station had contributed more than 60 reports to CNN prior to the 1991 change in government. For one of the *World Report* specials on refugees, ETV offered a news story picturing the half million refugees in the Sudan and an equal number in Kenya and Somalia. ETV frequently presented the government view of the Eutrean war and covered the story of the death of Mickey Leland, an American legislator who died in an air crash in Eastern Africa. CNN took the pictures from ETV via CNN's East Africa bureau in Nairobi.

Teshome Asrat, who produced *World Report* stories for Ethiopian television, explained that only recently were they able to make an equipment change from film cameras. Of the nine ENG cameras donated by an international organization, he said in 1990, only five are now working and one of these is at the President's office 'always'.

Seldom was ETV able to make use of the *World Report* stories of other countries in its own broadcasts. One of the problems was that the customs office placed a tax on the CNN cassettes as they arrived at the Addis Ababa airport, as many as 12 videotapes a month which cost the equivalent of US$50 each to clear them. The delay in getting tapes out of customs often ran up to 15 days.

Although research shows there is not just one answer to the question of why televison organizations are so intent on participating in the *CNN World Report* programme, what is clear is that CNN's desire to expand international coverage came at a time when nations were looking for the means to present their news and views to larger than domestic audiences. Having come to the conclusion, after 20 years of struggle and little to show for it, that the much-acclaimed New World Information and Communication Order was going nowhere, it's as if Third World broadcasters decided en masse they might as well join forces with a Western commercial broadcaster who would give them terms they could accept.

What CNN tapped into – both with its own staff and with TV journalists around the world – was a pool of unexploited talent, entrepreneurship and idealism. What CNN risked was its own hard-earned credibility using as news sources people not on its payroll and over whom it had neither managerial nor editorial control.

Gatekeeping

Another characteristic of *CNN World Report* that makes it quite different from other news organizations is the role of its editors. With *World Report* the editor's function is not that of the traditional gatekeeper deciding which stories get aired and which get cut. Rather, the editor's role is to keep the stories coming and, through creative packaging and promotion, keep the viewers viewing. The *World Report* editor worries less about a story being one-sided than about whether there are enough sides being aired to give the audience the widest possible perspective. Of course, the *World Report* editor has also to worry about the over-all look and long-term viability of this type of news service.

From the very first programme, the staff as well as some of the viewers were concerned the *World Report* would be flooded with self-promotional government-sponsored hype that would sacrifice journalistic neutrality and balance. The result would be, as one writer predicted, 'little old wood carver' stories from Eastern Europe and 'sun and fun on the beach' footage from the Caribbean. This did happen, and Stuart Loory was quoted as cautioning some of his contributors during the early days of the programme, 'If you continue to send stories like these (travelogues) people won't watch'.[6] Apparently, these concerns grew less and less, either because travelogues and woodcarver stories found an audience or because the *World Report* contributors adapted to CNN's expectations. The latter seems to be more the case.

Although requests for specific stories are not made, at least not for the weekend programme, the *World Report* staff say, 'A lot of time contributors like to get some type of feedback on the types of stories they are doing, or ideas on what we might think is interesting, but it's totally up to them. In terms of the weekend programme, what they contribute and whatever they send us, we air'.

'Good taste,' Loory told a columnist from the Phoenix, Arizona REPUBLIC in the week before *CNN World Report* premiered, 'to my way of thinking does not mean that we're going to keep everything off the air in which, say, the Iranians put on somebody ranting against the 'Great Satan' and Ronald Reagan. To me, that's news and views and information'. But he went on to clarify 'good taste does not include nudity and stuff like that'.[7]

Two years later, this definition was put to the test from an unusual source. Aleksey Denisov told of an incident in which a story sent from the USSR to *World Report* was rejected. Denisov is a 26-year-old anchor/reporter from a weekly programme of art and culture on TSS, the national television network of the former Soviet Union. What was offered was a story on the first sex festival in Moscow, seen by 60 million people on state television, in which there was erotic art, erotic games and a woman was made into a cake 'which the video showed the men licking her clean,' he said.

'We edited the show down to three minutes and sent it to CNN. Unfortunately, we cannot show it here, they say. In the USSR we were surprised. We are more perestroika than the USA,' he explained, apparently pleased with the turn of events. The *World Report* staff remember this incident a little differently. They say an erotic art show report from the Soviet Union was aired, so perhaps the Soviet contributors toned it down on their own before they submitted it.

The staff did recall an instance in which a segment was edited out of a story arriving by satellite from Cuba. In the judgement of the staff, had they aired it as it was the item could have brought a lawsuit against *World Report*. The Cuban report was about drug smuggling and included the address of one of those accused. 'They even showed exactly where on the street map his house was located,' Defending her actions, the *World Report* editor said, 'Even if a person is convicted of a crime, it should be illegal to publically announce the address of a culprit, since it would be a ticket to uninvited members of the public to retaliate against the person'.

An instance in which a questionable item was not edited was a story from Denmark on 'zone therapy,' a medical technique to ease the pain of labor and delivery. The opening shots of the news story showed in vivid close-up the birth of a baby. On American news, say the *World Report* staff, the scene would undoubtedly have been handled in a less direct way.

How does the contributor know what is acceptable to CNN? There are two answers to this question. The straightforward answer is that CNN will accept anything. There are no constraints other than the libel issues and the length of the story (no more than three minutes) laid out in the brief rules of the exchange. Contributing reporters and their agencies or governments are the first and only gatekeepers of content. The less-straight-forward answer is that what should be forwarded is '*CNN World Report*-type material'.

Contributors eventually figure it out. By talking to the *World Report* staff they get some clues: local stuff, human interest, what's happening regionally that will interest an international audience. They take clues from Ted Turner himself. While Turner has exercised no editorial control over *World Report*, his interest in environmental and peace issues is well-known. Contributors can look at CNN programming and get a reading. Clues can also be got from other contributors. Observing what is aired, what gets into the first 30 minutes of the newscast and what is reserved for the last hour, contributors are free to make their own decisions. According to the staff, 'they figure out its not really a question of what CNN wants, but what do they (the contributors) have to share with the rest of the world'.

The staff say stories with the greatest impact are not the ones about the news conferences and the diplomacy but about how people live. 'Keep in mind how little the American audience or the international audience know about what life is like in your country,' CNN writer Lori Waffenschmidt told a reporter from TV-3 Catalunya, Spain. 'We do appreci-ate very much the political reports that explain how the government operates and what conflicts there might be,' she said, 'but it is also very important to show what day care is like there, how people go to the grocery store, the cities and the countryside, things that show what your country is like, even if those things seem really mundane ...'.

With the advent of the daily *World Report*, or perhaps because of competitive pressures within CNN itself, there is now a push to get in more up-to-date stories. The staff ask contributors to give them stories of a more topical nature, when possible to cover breaking news from within their regions. 'The reason for this,' says Henry Schuster, an early producer with *World Report*, 'is that we feel that it enhances the programme'. Schuster was one of the first to look for ways to bring in more current news, allowing international contributors to give their perspectives on events that are just taking place.

Siobhan Darrow, a *World Report* producer that followed Schuster, continues the press for the breaking stories. At one of the meetings for contributors, she emphasized, 'When a story breaks in your country, we have several options. [We can] take a phone track from you. In other words, you write your story, you phone it in, it's yours editorially, and we use our video to cover it ... . Sometimes there is enough time for you to send a raw cassette, an uncut version, with a script we can track here. Or you can send up an analysis piece that we can update with you on the phone. Or take a story from your newscast – that is running on the air – and translate it for us. And if we are desperate enough, we might even take it untranslated and translate it here. If there's a breaking news story, call us, or we'll call you and figure something out'.

The telephone proved to be the key to getting in the up-to-date stories. During her time at *World Report*, Darrow says they were doing phone tracks almost every week. Often, as in the case with developments in Yugoslavia, the Baltic republics and the Soviet Union, contributors were asked to call in late Saturday night or Sunday morning. Their up-dated commentary was recorded and then covered with their own footage which had been submitted earlier, just in time for the Sunday afternoon show.

The *CNN World Report* staff work hard to keep the contributions coming, especially from under-represented regions of the world, to be supportive of reporters, encouraging, providing weekly telephone, telex and fax communications – as if the TV news broadcasters who contribute to *World Report* are members of their own staff in the field.

An example is the communication between Andrew Kelly of RTE-Ireland, who, in his weekly fax, asked for guidance. 'Due to crew availability, it would probably be possible for me to shoot two reports specially for CNNWR next week. However, we would have no use domestically for these so please advise today (Friday) if you want them, as they will have to be shot Monday for edit Tuesday and shipping Wednesday. If you can't get me today, try my home telephone number over the weekend (he gave his number in Dublin). I will be away in Spain Saturday, but leave a message on the answer phone'.

In his fax, Kelly described the two reports in detail, one of which involved an unusual monetary transaction between the USSR and Ireland in which in exchange for Ireland's setting up duty free shops in Moscow and Leningrad airports, Soviet Airline Aeroflot would send all its aircraft, the world's largest fleet, to Shannon Airport where they would be painted.

The decision is the reporter's but, in this case, the reporter's behavior reflected a more traditional journalist-station relationship. Kelly called in to see how his editor would react to his story proposal. He was seeking advice, if not a decision, from the *World Report* staff about what would work best. In this most unique of newscasts, the traditional roles persist.

Packaging

The *World Report* staff say they sometimes feel as if they are conducting a global correspondence course in TV news so much effort goes into working with contributors helping them improve the air quality of the stories submitted. Given their role, what sort of input and influence do CNN staff have in the final product?

The staff are clear about that. 'The content of the programme is determined by the contributors. What we have a say in is how the story sent to us is presented'. For example, Waffenschmidt notes, the staff decide which stories lead the programme and what goes into the second or third hour. If stories as delivered are over three minutes in length, the staff decide what to cut out, and they determine if something needs to be 'fixed' in a piece. They write the teasers and the introductions and select the visuals for the lead-ins, and worry about pacing, 'whatever is needed to make sure everything looks as best it can look that week'.

'Our job is to provide continuity through the programme,' Waffenschmidt replies. In answer to the question how much does CNN work over incoming material, she explains, 'We try to do a minimum amount. If the report comes in and the sound is okay and the video is okay, and you can follow the report, we don't touch it'.

But sometimes work has to be done to make the pieces airworthy. She notes 'satellite hits' – when audio or video is lost or garbled in transmission – that have to be repaired, mute pauses that must be taken out, SOTs (sound on tape) or interviews with people who are hard to understand must be subtitled, or dubbed into English when a different language is spoken or when the person's accent detracts. If changes are made it is within the context of always 'trying to keep in mind what the contributor wanted to do'.

With the audio, she notes, 'you can always transcribe what is said and say it yourself, improving the quality of the piece. We try to keep that to a minimum, (but) some pieces are in such difficult shape when they make it here'.

Contributions from Vietnam are among the hardest to understand, because of the poor technical quality of their reports and because of the accent. 'There is always a hard line to draw when something is difficult for you to understand – whether you accept that and air it in that form to get the flavor of the report, or if you have to re-voice it using (the voice of someone in Atlanta), you lose something. But at least then the ideas that country is trying to get across are clearly understood'.

When the contribution is over three minutes long 'we try to do the least amount we can to take out extraneous information to make sure that we're not taking out the meat of the report. Unless something is libelous or extremely offensive, we would never cut any content out of any piece that is under three minutes in length'.

For the anchor's introductions, staff writers try to provide the brief bit of background that is necessary for the audience to understand what is coming up in the report, or to call attention to any breaking news that may have happened since the report was assembled. To help the *World Report* staff prepare the wrap-around commentary, contributors are requested to provide, along with script and fonts, a suggested introduction and any other contextual material that might help the viewer to appreciate the story.

'We are trying to put as much video as possible into the shows,' the staff reminded contributors in one of their weekly fax communications. 'If you have good pictures for your story that were not used or the longer version of video that was used, please include them at the end of your package. We can use them in our video teases, promotions, and video slates. Also, if we do not have an updated picture of you, please include it in one of your shipments so we have it when we do phone interviews with you'. Contributors were told again, 'Another helpful item for our writers is a suggested introduction ... any information that you are not able to put in the report itself, or any additional or background information you have'.

Although the introductions are often one or two sentence lead-ins, sometimes more elaborate explanations are necessary. A July 1989 submission from Spain, on a political leader of an opposition party who was being released from jail, not only had a scripted introduction but included some video footage, drawn from the CNN video archive by the *World Report* writers, on the background to the events which led to his being jailed several years earlier. Because of internal-to-CNN copyright constraints, this practice of using CNN's own video in the *World Report* package has been discontinued.

When Armenia TV's regular contributor was in Atlanta for training, he was interviewed on the violence occuring along the Armenia/Azerbaijan border for the weekend programme. CNN file visuals and a map were used. Upon his return, his picture and a locator-map of the region was pulled up on the screen during daily *World Report* interviews.

In a May 1990 *CNN World Report* staff meeting chaired by Loory the staff went over again the principles of the exchange. Such meetings are necessary because, even though clearly stated as broad guidelines, the rules often require the exercise of judgement in practice because of their subtlety. On this day, the principle was reinforced that, for the week-end programme, tapes which are less than three minutes long are not to be edited unless there are mute pauses which can be taken out without altering the content. Tapes which are more than three minutes, staff members are reminded to 'cut from the contributor's point of view that will least hurt the telling of the story'.

In an instance when the staff had slightly changed the content of a story in re-voicing the tape 'to help the contributor' (the number of arrests was changed from four to three to reflect the apparent reality of the event), Loory had strong words. He said, 'It is not our mission to 'help' the contributors (by correcting their information). Once we start changing the content of filed stories, we are on dangerous ground'.

The staff also agreed that contributors should be informed of any actions taken which resulted in a change to the submitted piece by telephone, cable or fax, and a clear record entered into the computer (every staff member is connected to an easy-to-use desktop electronic mail system) to avoid misunderstandings and possible controversies.

The staff were cautioned that when different numbers appear on the news wires regarding casualties, or when wire information conflicts with a filed story from a *World Report* contributor, 'there is no guarantee that the wire stories are more reliable than the *World Report* stories'.

Once a news story has been aired on the weekend show, the daily staff can cut the story down as their wish. According to policy, the entire contribution has to be aired once in its entirety on one of the two shows. Thereinafter, the material is archived and made available for general use by CNN.

'News value' is the staff answer given to the question how do you decide what stories to package together. Positioning and the order of the line-up is an editorial judgement based on a sense of what pieces will play with one another, either because they have a common theme or because they represent a common geographical area. Increasingly, the lead stories are the breaking news stories followed by the feature material.

Waffenschmidt commented in an interview, 'For this week I have something on bungee jumping in Australia and I have something on rock-climbing in Singapore – a story on deaf rock climbers – so it's a kind of a nice little feature segment. Sometimes when all else fails, and there aren't (content) connections to be made, I have to figure out a way to work it together. Sometimes I might do some kind of regional grouping, putting together reports from Central America'.

In a February 1989 show there was a pairing of a story from the Bahamas with another from Singapore. In the Bahamas a 14-year old who operates a greeting card company is paying his mom US$5 an hour to help him with his business. In Singapore a 15-year old who keeps an aviary on the roof of his apartment building is selling birds for as much as US$500 per pair. In February 1990, a story from TV3-Catalunya on the effects of industrial waste on the Spanish landscape and air was paired with a CBC-Barbados story on contamination of the island's surface water by garbage dumping. In February 1991, a UAE-Abu Dhabi story on audiences staying close to their TV sets during the Persian Gulf crisis was matched with a similar story from CRTV-Cameroon.

The overall length of the programme is decided by the amount of material that arrives in time for the show. The merit of a 24-hour news service is that the window for news can be stretched to include a lot of material. Turner has made it clear to contributors and to *CNN World Report* staff the programme will be expanded up to 6 hours if needed, which is an indication of the priority given to *World Report* within CNN. A minimum of two hours is expected, for that is the afternoon time slot that must be filled. There have been several shows that have run more than three hours, a problem for the *World Report* crew who feel they aren't staffed to handle so much material in the time available.

References

1. Hank Whittemore, *CNN: The Inside Story*, Boston: Little, Brown and Company, 1990.
2. *Ibid.*
3. John P. Robinson and Mark Levy, *The Main Source: Learning From the News*, London: Sage, 1986.
4. Neil McManus, 'A New World View,' *Cable Choice*, June 1988.
5. Eli Flournoy, 'Daily World Report: An Analysis,' unpublished research report, Indiana University, Bloomington, 1991.
6. Bob King, 'The World of CNN,' *Journal Inquirer*, March 3, 1989.
7. Bud Wilkinson, '*World Report* Leaps high-tech, Language Barriers,' Phoenix, Arizona, *Republic*, November 10, 1987.

Chapter 3   WHAT MAKES THE NEWS?

'Subjects that were once regarded as arcane or not newsworthy are now prominently in the public eye'.
Javier Perez de Quellar, Former United Nations General Secretary, speaking of the *CNN World Report*

W hat kind of news is it?' This is one of the more interesting questions to ask of *World Report*. After 20 years of complaining about how poorly the news collected by international agencies reflects life in their countries, broadcasters of the developing world now have a chance to put the record straight. On CNN's *World Report* they can correct whatever misimpressions and fill in whatever gaps they see by reporting events from their own perspective. Guaranteed a slot on an internationally distributed network, what do the local stations have to say? Is it the same old news, or, is it news with a difference?

World Report content

Several studies conducted at Ohio University have addressed this question. Ganzert and Flournoy did a content analysis of weekend *World Report* newscasts of 1989, with follow-on studies for all of 1990 and half of 1991, sampling a full newscast every five weeks.[1,2] A rank order of the regions from which the stories came was derived, as was the percentage of total stories contributed by each region. For the 1989 period, 377 stories from 82 countries were examined; 601 stories from 94 nations were examined for 1990–91.

As Table 1 shows, Western European and Asian regions were the top contributors of stories to the *CNN World Report*. During the period sampled for 1989, for example, television news organizations in 15 Western European countries contributed stories, the largest contributors being West Germany and Switzerland. Together these two countries contributed 31 per cent of the stories from the region. Fifteen countries also contributed from Asia; the most frequent participants were Taiwan, Japan and Vietnam. These three nations had contributions in each of the 10 weeks sampled, totaling 43 per cent of the material aired from the Asian region.

37

Table 1. *World Report* stories aired by region and total countries that each region represents

	% of total stories		% of total countries	
Region	1989	1990–91	1989	1991–91
Western Europe	20	20	18	15
Asia	19	19	18	17
Middle	15	14	17	17
Latin America	15	11	23	25
Eastern Europe	13	14	7	10
Africa	12	15	12	12
Other	7	9	5	5

Among the stories originating from the Middle East, Afghanistan and Cyprus were the major contributors out of 14 nations. They accounted for 35 per cent of the total stories from that region. Cuba and Nicaragua were the largest contributors among the 19 participating nations of Latin America. They contributed 31 per cent of all stories from the region. The Soviet Union accounted for 21 per cent of the total stories contributed among the six participating countries of Eastern Europe.

The 1990–91 up-date using a larger 16-week sample reflected similar patterns, with some noteworthy differences. Western Europe and Asia continued to lead the field in terms of total number of stories contributed. Middle East contributions fell off slightly (even when the sample included the time period of the crisis in the Persian Gulf) and Latin American participation fell to near the bottom. Eastern European representation increased, as did Africa. Africa moved from sixth to third place in total number of stories contributed.

Ganzert and Flournoy compared their data to the results of a 1984 study by Weaver *et al.* of 'Patterns in Foreign News Coverage on US Network TV: A Ten Year Analysis'.[3] Although the time-frame of these studies is not parallel, the comparisons are nevertheless instructive, especially in considering the types of news carried on the *CNN World Report* compared with those which have been carried on the US television networks.

As shown in Table 2, some similarities and some differences appear. For example, the amount of foreign relations and domestic relations news – in some studies referred to as political news – was almost identical when the news offerings of the two services were compared. Foreign relations and domestic relations were the second and third-ranked categories. The first-ranked categories, on the other hand, were not at all similar. The greatest number of stories carried by ABC, CBS and NBC during the sample period fell into military/ national defence categories (ranked sixth on *World Report*); the greatest number of stories carried by *World Report* in the 1989 sample fell into a category called arts/culture (ranked thirteenth in the Weaver study of the US networks). Ecology/environment ranked fifth on *World Report* and sixteenth on the US networks.

In 1990–91, domestic news emerged as the type of story most frequently aired on the *CNN World Report* followed by foreign relations and economics. The arts/culture stories and those addressing ecology/environment and science/health were still prominent on

World Report but there was an increased amount of military/defence news. Although distinctive in some respects, in terms of topical content, *World Report* news began to look more like the international news of other services.

Noteworthy, though, is the fact that while 75 per cent of the international news carried by the US networks was concentrated into only four topical categories, namely military/defence, foreign and domestic relations and crime/justice, only 35 per cent of *World Report* news was of this type in 1989. That percentage was 43 per cent in 1990–91. The *CNN World Report* thus represents a fuller range of possible news, including the less-well-addressed issues of religion, science, ecology, education and race and ethnic relations. In practice, the definition of what is news and what is newsworthy is broader on *World Report*.

Table 2. Comparison of topics and percentage of stories appearing by topical category

	US Networks	CNN *Wolrld Report*	
Topic	1984	1989	1990–91
Military/Defence	1 (26%)	6 (7%)	5 (7%)
Foreign Relations	2 (23%)	2 (12%)	2 (12%)
Domestic Relations	3 (16%)	3 (11%)	1 (18%)
Crime/Justice	4 (10%)	7 (6%)	8 (6%)
Economics	5 (5%)	8 (6%)	3 (5%)
Human Interest	6 (4%)	9 (6%)	10 (5%)
Miscellaneous	7 (3%)	4 (8%)	9 (6%)
Prominent Persons	8 (3%)	11 (3%)	12 (3%)
Natural Disasters	9 (2%)	17 (1%)	16 (3%)
Labour/Wages	10 (2%)	16 (2%)	18 (0%)
Sports	11 (1%)	15 (2%)	11 (3%)
Accidents	12 (1%)	18 (0%)	17 (1%)
Arts/Culture	13 (1%)	1 (18%)	4 (8%)
Race/Ethnic	14 (1%)	12 (3%)	13 (2%)
Religion	15 (1%)	13 (2%)	14 (2%)
Ecology/Agriculture	16 (1%)	5 (7%)	6 (7%)
Education	17 (0%)	14 (2%)	15 (2%)
Science/Health	18 (0%)	10 (5%)	7 (6%)

Note: all percentages rounded

Another Ohio University study, an examination of development news on *CNN World Report* by Rani Dilawari *et al.*, found that of the 308 separate news items appearing in a randomly chosen sample of 10 weekly newscasts during 1989, 61 per cent were development-oriented stories.[4] That is, they were stories having less to do with politics, defence, military, crime, conflict and disaster and more to do with economic activities, social services, culture, science and health and items of human interest.

Compared with a study undertaken for the International Association for Mass Communication Research (IAMCR) under the direction of Sreberny-Mohammadi in 1985, the Dilawari team found significant differences. The IAMCR study combined research of foreign news reports in the media of 29 countries and a study of eight services of the four major wire agencies. When compared, the results showed that almost three-quarters of the big four wire agency stories and two-thirds of the domestic media stories related to national and domestic politics, military, defence, crime and disaster, while only about one-third of the *World Report* stories addressed such topics.

The emphasis in the *CNN World Report*, when taken as a whole, was on a broader range of topics relating to the economy, to international aid, social services, arts and culture, science and technology, health and medicine, ecology and human interest. Almost 50 per cent of *World Report* stories related to such topics, against 22 per cent carried on the wire agencies and 25 per cent on the local media.

The research team also found that the proportion of development news from stations in developing countries was slightly higher (51 per cent) than from stations in developed countries (49 per cent). This is perhaps not a surprising result but it should be noted that the sample analysed in this research included more stories from developing countries (n = 167) than from developed countries (n = 141). As a proportion of their respective contributions to *CNN World Report* stations in developed countries actually contributed a higher percentage of development news (65 per cent) than did developing countries (56 per cent).[5]

A study by Park *et al.*, which examined 566 *World Report* stories submitted by a total of 106 broadcast news organizations from 96 countries during 1990–91, also found some important differences in the amount of development news contributed by developed and developing countries.[6] In the presentation of domestic news (news concerning the internal issues of a country) both the developed and the developing countries focused more on development news than on non-development news. Yet, both the developed and developing countries oriented their coverage more toward non-development news in what they offered as international news (news involving two or more nations). Park found that, in respect to international news, the Western media tended to contribute more development news.

In fact, when examining studies on *World Report* content beginning in 1987, a decreasing trend in the proportion of development news contributed by the developing countries was noted. The proportion of development news from the developing world was 67 per cent in 1987–88. This fell to 58 per cent in 1989 and to 52 per cent in 1990–91. This occurred while the proportion of development news in *CNN World Report*, as a whole, was falling from 65 per cent in 1987–88 to 60 per cent in 1989 to 57 per cent in 1990–91. Yet, the proportion of development (compared to non-development) news contributed by the developed countries actually increased during this same period, from 60 per cent to 65 per cent to 63 per cent.

Park concludes, 'If *CNN World Report* is an example of the ideal NIICO newscast – in which countries are free to present their own news from their own perspectives – we may be seeing a new trend in the use of development journalism by both developed and developing countries. Namely, development news is as likely to come from the North as well as the South, the affluent as well as the poorer nations of the world'.

The Dilawari study also looked at the types of stations participating in the *CNN World Report*, e.g. those which were owned and operated by the government, those which were government-owned and independently operated and those which were privately-owned and operated. This was no easy item to investigate due to structural/political/economic changes going on in many of the contributing countries during this time frame, but it mattered little since no significant differences were found in terms of development news offered. On the average, the government-affiliated stations were the ones contributing a slightly higher proportion of development news on *CNN World Report.*

The Dilawari and the Park studies both noted that the most frequently seen actors in the *World Report* news tended to be government spokespersons and politicians. Park noted that developing countries tended to give greater visibility to politicians and government officials. This result was consistent with the earlier IAMCR findings. On the *World Report*, however, a significantly larger percentage of scientific and academic people and common citizens also appeared.

Ingrid D. Volkmer, a German researcher, examined Sunday editions of *World Report* for four weeks of July and August 1990. About 30 per cent (33 of 112) topics covered in her sample were political, by far the greatest number. Ecology (15) and culture (15) topics were second and third most common, followed by military (11) topics. Twelve per cent of the news originated from African countries; 46 per cent of the African reports addressed political issues. On a measure of good news/bad news, the number of positive and negative events covered were almost equally divided. As she reports, 'The slogan 'only bad news are good news' seems to be not appropriate for *World Report*'.[7]

Volkmer concluded that *CNN World Report* has become a forum for exchanging news that is not soft but 'hard'. This was contrary to predictions, especially among those who view Third World journalism as mostly apolitical news of the 'development type,' reflecting government initiative, pressure or outright censorship. She also found that in 16 reports (14 per cent) the country of the broadcast station and the country of the event did not correspond. That is, the contributing station was covering news happening in a country other than its own.

In the 1990–91 up-date of their earlier study, Ganzert and Flournoy looked at the instances of stations covering or commenting on news events occuring in other countries or regions. Of the 601 stories included in their sample, 96 of these were not station reports on their own country. Of these, only 14 were examples of traditional centre-to-periphery news agencies sending crews out to cover news events wherever they happen around the world. Examples appearing in the sample were FR3-France reporting on events in Somalia, the BBC reporting on Japan, Deutsche Welle-Germany reporting on South Africa and CNN sending in a story from Panama.

Twenty five of the 96 news events originated with the lesser-known stations, often reporting periphery-to-periphery, such as Network 10-Australia reporting on New Zealand, ZBC-Zimbabwe reporting on Tanzania, CCTV-China reporting on North Korea, BT-Bulgaria reporting on India, Pakistan TV reporting on Bangladesh and TRT-Turkey reporting on Iraq.

Fifteen of the stories represented the type of reverse reporting arrangements seldom seen on Western television – that is, from periphery-to-centre. These were reports originating with TTV-Taiwan covering events on mainland China, with Mongolia TV commenting on events in the USSR, JRT-Jordan reporting on events in France, CST-Czechoslovakia looking at Austria, IRTC-Cuba reporting on Brazil and TV Asahi-Japan reporting on the USA.

The largest number, thirty nine, were contributions from transnational or non-national news organizations such as UNTV-United Nations, which had its reporters in Guatamala one week and in Namibia the next. Also included were Globalvision, an organization headquartered in New York but giving attention to events in southern Africa, the Afghan Media Resource Center (AMRC), a rebel political group operating out of Pakistan but covering events in Afghanistan, and PLO-TV which comments on events in the Middle East from its base in Tunis.

Another group of contributors, not falling within the definition given above, are those representing the successionist states of the USSR and of Yugoslavia. *World Report* stories were coming from Armenia, Estonia, Latvia, Lithuania, Croatia, Sarajevo and Slovenia as if they were independent countries. In point of fact, since the news sample was taken, most of these countries have become independent. *World Report* was one of the ways they communicated their progress toward independence to the rest of the world.

LuEtt Hanson, Kent State University, examined images of women in the *CNN World Report*.[8] Her sample consisted of three newscasts drawn from September, October and November 1990. Among the 90 news reports examined, there were 137 appearances by newsmakers – defined as a person visible on the screen and identified by name or title in the audio or by a super – 120 (88 per cent) of whom were male. Only 12 per cent of *World Report* newsmakers were female and most of them appeared as private individuals.

In the Hanson study, the largest number of male newsmakers showed up in stories about foreign relations/diplomacy and military/national defence. These two categories together accounted for 28 per cent of all male appearances. Foreign relations and defence were also two of the four topic categories having the most stories – the other two were arts/culture/entertainment and economics/business.

The largest numbers of female newsmakers appeared in stories from Western Europe, from Africa, and from the 'other' category which consisted of transnational news organizations such as UNTV-United Nations. No women newsmakers appeared in the Latin American stories sampled, with only a handful showing up in stories from Asia, Eastern Europe and the Middle East.

Eighty nine of the 90 stories in this study were told by a reporter. Fifty three (60 per cent) of the reporters were male and 36 (40 per cent) were female. The regions where more women were reporters than men were Asia and Latin America. Western Europe had three times as many male reporters as women. The largest number of female reporters appeared in stories about arts/culture/entertainment; the lowest proportion of female reporters was in economics/business.

Hansen comments 'It is disheartening to see how similar the images of women in *CNN World Report* are to the images of women in American news programmes'. She cites a 1977 US Commission on Civil Rights study which found that male newsmakers outnumbered female newsmakers by almost nine to one in TV newscasts, 'the same ratio that exists in *CNN World Report*'. The representation of women as news reporters in the CNN programme she found 'much more encouraging'.

Hansen acknowledges the limitations of her study, a too-modest sample drawn within a too-constricted time frame. Also, the timing of the study which coincided with the military build-up in the Persian Gulf may have overly influenced the results. A more recent study by Dilawari *et al.* with a much larger sample (15 weekend reports of 1990 and 1991) shows that the ratio of male to female reporters noted by Hansen is right on-target, while the gap between male and female actors appearing on the *CNN World Report* is actually wider than reported.[9]

Of 1321 main and subsidiary actors appearing on *World Report*, only 233 (18 per cent) were female. Only 63 (4 per cent) of the women actors appeared as main actors – that is, as primary newsmakers. Of these, only 14 appeared in their capacity as politician, governmental or political official. Only nine women appeared as cultural, scientific, academic or technical experts.

Out of a total of 524 reporters, 206 (39 per cent) were women and 318 (61 per cent) were men. The surprising result is that the per cent of women reporters from the developing world (66 per cent, n = 136) was twice that for the developed countries (33 per cent, n = 68). Among the developing countries contributing news to the CNN programme, there was an almost equal representation of women (50 per cent, n = 136) and men (50 per cent, n = 134). In terms of regions, Asia (54 per cent) and the Middle East (55 per cent) accounted for more women than men reporters.

Previous research had shown that very few women were involved in the coverage of stories about international and domestic politics, military/defence, crime and disasters. The Ohio University research shows that, in contrast, a near-equal proportion of men (35 per cent) and women (33 per cent) reporters covered these topics in the *CNN World Report*.

Daily *World Report*

The daily *World Report* is a special case. The CNN staff have complete control over which stories are aired. Only about 20 minutes have been set aside within the International Hour for *World Report* news and, with commercial advertisements, even less time is actually available. Unlike the weekly show, daily producers solicit reports on specific topics. Editorial content is still up to contributors but not everything that comes in is used. Stories run in a format that sometimes departs from that used on weekends.

On the daily *World Report* all of the following approaches are used: (1) reports aired on the previous weekend programme (or those just arrived intended for an up-coming programme; (2) especially prepared reports sent by contributors in time for the 3:00 EST International Hour; (3) telephoned reports from contributors that have been pre-recorded and covered with video from the *World Report* library; and (4) live interviews, via phone or satellite or within the Atlanta studio, with contributing reporters. On most days, a maximum of five reports are aired, generally ranging from one to three minutes in length.

In 1990, a study was done by Eli Flournoy of 12 consecutive weeks of the daily programme. His objective was to determine which news organizations had stories airing on the daily *World Report*, how equally were the regions of the world represented by news on the daily *World Report*, how regional coverage on the daily programme compared to regional coverage on the US networks, and which topics were most frequently covered on the daily programme compared with the networks.[10]

The sample covered 222 reports from 73 contributors from 56 countries. Table 3 gives an abbreviated listing (those with four or more contributions) in rank order of the total number of stories each news organization had aired on the daily *World Report* during the period of the study. Thirty per cent of all reports aired came from five contributors: SABC-South Africa, Deutche Welle-West Germany, UNTV-United Nations, Global TV-Canada and BBC-United Kingdom. The top five contributors, except for SABC-South Africa, were all Western-based agencies.

Table 3. Contributors to the daily *CNN World Report*: 12 May – 5 August 1990

Contributing news organizations	Number of reports
SABC-South Africa	21
Deutsche Welle-West Germany	15
UNTV-United Nations	12
Global TV-Canada	10
BBC-United Kingdom	9
TV Asahi-Japan	8
SRI-TV-Switzerland	8
RNTV-Netherlands	6
SBC-Singapore	6
TRT-Turkey	6
ABS-CBN-Philippines	5
BT-Bulgaria	5
YLE-Finland	5
GBC-Ghana	4
Globalvision-South Africa	4
Jordan TV-Jordan	4
SVT1-Sweden	4
Network 10-Australia	4
TSS-Soviet Union	4

The Western European region led in total number of stories, in number of contributing news organizations and in number of countries participating. Africa and Asia were not far behind in number of countries participating, although they generated fewer stories. SABC tended to dominate the contributions from Africa; it had 21 out of 40 reports aired. Its nearest competitor from the African region was GBC-Ghana with four reports.

Eastern Europe had one-third the stories of Western Europe and half the number of countries contributing. Latin American stations contributed even fewer stories, although the number of Latin American countries offering one or more news items was larger than those from Eastern Europe or the Middle East. (It should be noted that this news sample was taken from 12 May – 5 August 1990, before the impact of the Iraqi invasion of Kuwait was fully felt.)

This research, which was shared with the *World Report* staff, led to internal discussions of policy and eventually to changes in procedures in the daily programme. In December 1991, a follow-up study was done by Don Flournoy at the request of Donna Mastrangelo, newly appointed executive producer for *World Report*.[11] 'I would venture to say you will now find the reports more balanced,' she predicted. Mastangelo wanted the research up-dated because she thought a new sample would show less reliance on a few highly-productive contributors and a more even geographic distribution.

The new sample examined seven consecutive months of daily *World Report* programming (May through November 1991). The much larger sample included 90 contributors from 76 countries producing an estimated 520 stories. (Note: an exact number of stories cannot be given because of occasional pre-emptions of the International Hour by the network for such breaking news stories as the assassination of Rajiv Ghandi and continuous coverage of the US confirmation hearings of CIA director Robert Gates and Supreme Court justice Clarence Thomas.)

Table 4. Comparison of topics aired between US networks and daily *CNN World Report*

	US Networks	Daily *CNN Wolrld Report*
Topic	1984	1990
Military/Defence	1 (26%)	3 (10%)
Foreign Relations	2 (23%)	2 (15%)
Domestic Relations	3 (16%)	1 (15%)
Crime/Justice	4 (10%)	8 (5%)
Economics	5 (5%)	4 (8%)
Human Interest	6 (4%)	16 (1%)
Natural Disasters	7 (3%)	12 (3%)
Prominent Persons	8 (3%)	13 (2%)
Sports	9 (2%)	6 (7%)
Race/Ethnic	10 (2%)	9 (5%)
Art/Culture	11 (1%)	7 (6%)
Education	12 (1%)	14 (2%)
Labour/Wages	13 (1%)	15 (2%)
Ecology/Environment	14 (1%)	5 (8%)
Accidents	15 (1%)	17 (0%)
Science/Health	16 (1%)	11 (3%)
Religion	17 (0%)	18 (0%)
Miscellaneous	18 (0%)	8 (7%)

Research showed that SABC-South Africa (28), the BBC (22), Deutsche Welle (21) and United Nations TV (16) were still among the top five contributors, but their contributions were down proportionately. The number one contributor for 1991 had become Yugoslavia, a little-seen contributor in the earlier sample. The five Yugoslavian stations (Serbia, Croatia, Slovenia, Montenegro and Sarajevo) contributed 69 of the 520 stories for the period. TSS-Soviet Union (14), LBC-Lebanon (11), TRT-Turkey (11) and CRT-Cameroon (10) were also among the top 10 contributors, with 77 additional stations generating the other stories. When comparing regional coverage by the daily *World Report* with the Weaver study, 'Patterns in Foreign News Coverage on US Network TV: a 10-Year Analysis,' Eli Flournoy found little difference of significance. As can be seen in Table 4, domestic relations, international relations and military/defence were the top ranked topics on both services. Economic issues were given attention by both. The daily *World Report* tended to give somewhat more emphasis to ecology/agriculture and arts/culture issues while the US Networks gave more attention to crime/justice. On the other hand, the networks had more human interest stories and the daily *CNN World Report* programme carried more sports.[12]

The daily programme of *World Report*, although emphasizing breaking news, gives attention nevertheless to a wide range of news topics. Like the news appearing on the *World Report* weekend programme, the daily programme tends to cover news in a greater number of categories than did the US Networks in earlier studies noted. A broad contributor base is also drawn on but the daily *World Report* in the sampled period was clearly relying on a few very sophisticated news services to supply it with the bulk of its news.

World Report Specials

An interesting exception to *World Report* rules is the *World Report* 'special'. From time to time, the CNN staff solicit stories centering on a theme for special reports within the weekend programme. The frequency of these, along with the mini-specials called 'segments,' appear to be growing and may become a regular feature. The first *World Report* special appeared during the Christmas holidays 1987. International contributors were asked to submit stories – where appropriate – about how Christmas was celebrated in their countries.

Afterward, a reader wrote CNN to say it was a 'wonderful coming together' appreciating the fact that there was 'no criticism, ridiculing, jealousy or finger pointing among those reporting, only a 'this is what we do at Christmas and we want to share'.' She liked the fact that no one seemed to have their guard up and wished the entire programme could be made available to children. 'Wouldn't it be fantastic to plant some good seeds,' she said.

Forty-seven reports were aired on the AIDS special in December 1988. The programme ran three hours and 16 minutes, which broke all records for length in the weekend programme. Several additional AIDS pieces arrived too late for inclusion and were used in a special segment on the following Sunday. According to the *CNN World Report* staff, there were lots of phone calls from viewers after, requesting a rerun of the programme or information about one aspect or another of the programme.

The June 1989, *World Report* special segment on abortion was probably the show that elicited the most viewer mail and phone calls. Thirteen stories were aired from such countries as Argentina, Egypt, India, the Philippines, Poland and Zimbabwe. One angry viewer wrote, 'What we experienced today could well have been entitled 'The International Planned Parenthood Propaganda Hour' ... really why wasn't it? ... As a Catholic I found this programme offensive'.

Other viewers agreed, 'Your entire segment was both biased and disrespectful ... I thought we could turn to you for news, but now I know differently ... . Please handle the power you possess with care ... don't let pro-abortionists snow you. In your heart and soul, you know the truth. Please stick to it'.

As an experiment, on the following weekend, one of the letter writers was given the chance to state his views on the air. In a prepared statement which he read, the viewer gave examples of 'factual errors and distortions' he found in the broadcast and described the programme as 'something shoveled out from Planned Parenthood's propaganda mills'.

Letters also came from the other side. Following the showing of the abortion segment a man from New Jersey wrote, 'Your Sunday programme is what television is all about. You present real information, not petty robberies, or rent strikes and such. I also catch your programme overseas. God Bless Ted Turner. By not playing it safe, he's changing the whole television medium. More than half my watching time is spent with CNN. You are the real 'Voice of America'.' He added, 'P.S. Just remember, keep a proper balance between commercials and content. The networks are killing me with too long and too frequent commercials'.

Thirteen news organizations reported for the August 1989, special programme on the Non-Aligned Movement, which provided perspectives on the history and development of NAM and previews of the upcoming meeting in Belgrade. Once again experimenting, JRT-Yugoslavia assumed responsiblity as co-producer with CNN for this one-hour special segment. TV Ljubljana's Blanka Dobersek served as co-host with Ralph Wenge.

Twenty-eight television news organizations submitted stories for a December 1989, special on Refugees and the Homeless. In a programme entitled *Nobody Wants Me*, which won an award in the Houston International Film and Video Festival, reports focused on why people become refugees due to war, political conflict and natural disasters. The pieces also looked at the impact of refugee populations on the societies where they seek asylum, at life in refugee camps and immigration policies and successful solutions to refugee pressures. Other reports focused on street people and programmes to house them.

A more technologically sophisticated segment was the one on German reunification in October 1990. Co-anchored with Siegfried Berndt, Deutsche Welle Television, the programme incorporated a live panel of scholars in a four-way satellite hook-up between Bonn, Moscow, Washington D.C. and Atlanta. East German TV had prepared a historical perspective on the partitioning of the country, including segments on the 1961 construction of the Berlin wall and its subsequent fall in November 1989. DDF-Germany and FR 3-France contributed stories as did SVT-Sweden and Radio Netherlands TV.

In April 1991, in making plans for a special on Religion and Ethnicity, the *World Report* staff included the following in their weekly fax communication to contributing stations. 'We are very interested in covering the various conflicts around the world that have roots in religious or ethnic differences. These could be economic, political or social conflicts in your countries. Has historical or recent immigration aggravated these problems? What role does language play and what does the future hold? Also, are there cases in your country where these problems have been solved peacefully? Please note that we will be devoting the entire 26 May programme to this topic. Because of the the number of reports we expect to receive, we ask that you send them to us to arrive by 17 May. Please let us know whether you will be able to contribute a report to this special'.

When the programme ran, 37 stories had been submitted. Typical of these was a story on the long-standing conflict between Muslims and Christians on the Philippine island of Mindanao, a story on racial violence against Aborigines in Australia, on skinheads' attacks on foreigners in Germany, territorial and ethnic disputes between the Soviet republics of Armenia and Azerbaijan, clashes between Croats and Serbs in Yugoslavia, nationalist movements in the Basque Country of Spain, conflicts between Moslems and Buddhists in Sri Lanka, religion in the politics of Cameroon, Quebec sucession and the 500th anniversary of Jews in Turkey. The lead story was the news story of the week: the assasination of Rajiv Gandhi.

In response to a March 1991 special segment on Ramadan celebrations around the globe, to which such countries as Egypt, Jordan, Quatar, Saudi Arabia, Singapore and Syria participated, CNN received the following letter: 'Dear CNN: As an Arab-Muslim, I would like to thank you for your unbiased and informative report on the holy month of Ramadan. To the Arabs, it is extremely important that our culture and religion be portrayed in a positive manner. I encourage more reports like these to help others understand the meaning of Islam and in addition, to clear any misconceptions about our culture'.

References

1. Charles Ganzert and Don Flournoy, 'An Analysis of CNN's Weekly *World Report* Program, *Journalism Quarterly*, Spring, 1992.

2. Don Flournoy and Chuck Ganzert, '*CNN World Report*: 1990–91 Research,' Research Monograph, Institute for Telecommunications Studies, Ohio University, Athens, Ohio, 1992.

3. Ganzert, 1992.

4. Rani Dilawari, Robert Stewart and Don Flournoy, 'Development News on *CNN World Report*, *Gazette*, 47: 121-137, 1991.

5. *Ibid.*

6. Chun-il Park, Rani Dilawari and Don Flournoy, 'Development Orientation of Domestic and International News on the *CNN World Report*,' Research Monograph, Institute for Telecommunications Studies, Ohio University, Athens, Ohio, 1992.

7. Ingrid Volkmer, 'CNN and the Globalization of Knowledge,' unpublished paper, Universitat Bielefeld, F.R.Germany, 1991.

8. LuEtt Hanson, 'Images of Women in *CNN World Report*,' paper presented at the Broadcast Education Association convention, Las Vegas, April 1991.

9. Rani Dilawari, Chun-il Park and Don Flournoy, 'Women on the *CNN World Report*: Reporters and Actors in International Television News,' Research Monograph, Institute for Telecommunications Studies, Ohio University, Athens, Ohio, 1992.

10. Eli Flournoy, 'Daily World Report: An Analysis,' unpublished research report, Indiana University, Bloomington, 1991.

11. Don Flournoy, 'CNN Daily World Report: 1991 Research,' Research Monograph, Institute for Telecommunications Studies, Ohio University, Athens, Ohio, 1992.

12. Eli Flournoy, 1991.

Chapter 4   THE ORIGINS OF *CNN WORLD REPORT*

'A few years ago Cameroonians didn't know what TV was. Now you find satellite dishes all over the place'.
Eric Chinje, Correspondent for CRTV Cameroon

As an international newscast and news exchange, *World Report* is unprecedented in terms of its scope, the diversity and balance of its coverage and in the nature of its content. As such, it represents a dramatic shift in the historic pattern of international news content and news flow.

The research shows that more countries are participating in the effort than ever have been involved in any single news collection and distribution enterprise in history. The topics covered are more varied and their treatment pursued to greater depth, with fewer regions of the world neglected. Even with no formal contracts with CNN and no hope of compensation, local broadcasters are sending their news in to *World Report*. Why? What is the motivating force behind this development?

It would be easy to assume that the world's first 'ya all come' news show is in place because of the unorthodox personal and business philosophy of Ted Turner. In this case, Turner is the man with the idea and the financial means to mount such a service, but Turner did not create the conditions which made *World Report* possible. Timing, politics, economics and advancements in technology all helped set the stage for the *World Report* venture. Technological factors, such as telephones that work, easier access to satellites and hand-held cameras and computers have allowed for more timely and cost effective communication. The emergence of a political climate for freer use of the media and the easing of restrictions on the flow of electronic information across national borders played a role. At the same time, there was an apparent rising public demand for unfiltered news, while local broadcasters were themselves anxious to get their stories aired to broader publics. Without these forces at work it is unlikely that the *World Report*, or any such egalitarian news arrangement, would have yet appeared in the international arena.

Information technologies

News sharing had to be technically feasible for *World Report* to emerge. The strategic technologies in this case were the global information networks, in particular the satellite linkages which allow the regions of the world to talk easily back and forth and the new electronic news gathering equipment, the new cameras and editing machines, which permit production of broadcast quality pictures on a more modest budget. Also key are the cable and other outlets which can now make use of an increased amount of international news.

News traffic among the major centres of the world, north and south, now rides easily on electronic highways that branch across the world map. The technical bases of this new access to the channels of communication are the microelectronics, computer and telecommunication systems which make news gathering and distribution faster, more economical and more user-friendly. Breakthroughs in the technologies have made it possible for individuals as well as nations to become more self-sufficient, to produce and distribute their own voice, video and data communications.

When Ghana's president Jerry Rawlings announced he was sending troops into Liberia in the Summer 1990, the only news coming from the region came from wire reports. With satellite phone linkages, *CNN World Report* was able to receive an audio report from Ghana Broadcasting Corporation, add video from its archive and broadcast it to the world – within minutes. For journalists, access to global technologies means that they are virtually able to communicate, no matter where they are, whenever they want with whomever they desire.

The growth of compatible information networks has set the stage for a more balanced flow and more equitable participation in international news collection and distribution. For the first time in history a borderless telecommunication system connecting nations is close to reality. This is a basic condition for news sharing. Admittedly, access to international news pipelines is still inequitably distributed. The channels of communication are not affordable by all, or available to all the political out-groups, but the terminals are now there in-country and local staff have been trained to manage them without outside help. International telecommunications standards are being set which make it possible for formerly incompatible communication systems to interlink.

In Asia, for example, international standard fibre optic lines, sponsored by AT&T and others, are already in place along high traffic corridors. These high capacity channels, using light impulses rather than analog electrical waves, are replacing the slower interference-prone copper telephone and telex cables. They also reduce the need for microwave towers and will eventually compete with satellites for video exchanges. A new fibre cable system connecting the Philippines, Guam, Japan and Hawaii to North America with a Pacific channel capable of 40,000 simultaneous telephone calls or more than 40 uncompressed television programmes is now being installed.[1]

Australia and New Zealand also are being linked to the North American continent with the largest submarine cable network ever built, about 15,150 miles of fibre optic cable. The Australia-New Zealand link will provide 57,000 voice circuits, compared to the 480 channels the TASMAN 1 cable currently provides.[2]

Two-way satellite communication is now possible from almost any point on the globe. There are few countries left which do not use satellites in some form. Domestic use within countries such as China, Japan, Indonesia, Brazil, and Mexico is widespread. Intelsat, the international satellite consortium to which about 140 countries of the world belong, not only provides the means for in-country distribution of voice and data and video signals, it is the link which almost all nations now use for electronic communication with the rest of the world. Intelsat manages 16 ocean-bridging satellites world-wide. As a non-profit cooperative it can provide a rate structure which encourages participation of low-use nations using its profits from high traffic corridors.

Up to the time of the change of government in Ethiopia in May 1991, ETV-Ethiopia had submitted more than 60 stories to *World Report* for distribution and use within the CNN news exchange. According to Wole Gurmu, director general of Ethiopian TV, it was cheaper for him to send his stories to Atlanta by cassette (about US$100) than to send them by satellite (about US$600). But it was less of a headache and faster when he could up-link the news directly from his country on the Intelsat service. With the satellite he didn't have the hassle of customs nor the delays and the risk of airline routing. Via satellite he could send breaking news.

Regional news exchanges

The realization that local news organizations are capable of contributing stories for international distribution and that there is a market for such material, grew out of the satellite-based regional news exchanges.

The first of these exchanges, outside of superpower control, began in 1982 under the sponsorship of the Organisation Internationale de Radiodiffusion et Télévision. Headquartered in Prague, OIRT was a primarily Eastern European consortium of 14 active members and five receive-only sites that included the German Democratic Republic, Hungary, Poland, Bulgaria, Romania, and the USSR. Cuba, Yugoslavia, Australia and Finland also participated.[3]

OIRT service, called Intervision, began as a means for exchanging locally produced television programmes using the Intersputnik network of the USSR. Since Intervision participants also belonged to the Intersputnik system, news items transmitted via Intelsat from London to Moscow could be relayed via Intersputnik to Intervision countries, and back again. By 1990, over 7000 items of news had been exchanged.

In April 1984, a group of Asian countries, including India, Pakistan, Bangladesh, Sri Lanka, Brunei, Malaysia and Indonesia, began exchanging television news stories once each week via the Pacific Ocean and Indian Ocean Intelsat networks with Kuala Lumpur as the centre. At about the same time, the People's Republic of China, the Republic of Korea, Japan, Hong Kong, Australia and New Zealand entered into a similar agreement with Tokyo serving as the coordinating link.

These were countries with diverse – sometimes conflicting – cultural and political backgrounds and very different technical systems. All three television line standards (625 PAL, 625 SECAM and 525 NTSC) were represented among them. In some cases, as with China and Korea, news was being exchanged even while diplomatic relations and trade were severely constrained.

51

In spite of the handicaps, these news exchanges have been remarkably successful in Asia and now operate on a daily schedule. Local news editors, following a clearly understood principle that each is free to offer whatever stories it likes and that each is free to receive or refuse any story offered, look for news items that might be of interest to others within the network. For the most part, the news items that were traded on the satellite were those originally collected for local consumption.

Sometimes it happened, as with the Bhopal disaster in India, the story was first covered by the local news team, shared with the Asiavision news exchange and picked up by Eurovision or Visnews for international distribution. This happens much more frequently today, with stories credited to AVN now appearing on the evening news programmes of many nations.

In 1985, a project of the Arab States Broadcasting Union led to the launching of a satellite to serve 22 Arab countries. Saudi Arabia, Libya and Egypt picked up more than 50 per cent of the cost of the Arabsat regional satellite system, with much smaller contributions coming from countries such as Morocco, Tunisia and Algeria. Arabsat was conceived as a way to promote Arab unity, assist in economic development and facilitate cultural cooperation.

Today, Arabsat is somewhat in disarray. It provides for telecommunications, weather information gathering, and a few television programme exchanges such as the transmitting of sports events between Saudi Arabia and the Gulf States (Kuwait, United Arab Emirates, Bahrain, Quatar, Oman). Before the Gulf war, political differences were given as the principal reason the system had not become a significant programme source for local stations. It remains to be seen whether countries such as Egypt, Saudi Arabia and the Gulf States, which traditionally have been allies of the USA, will find common ground for a working news exchange with countries such as Syria, Algeria, and Libya, which had aligned themselves politically with the USSR.

In 1991 a parallel exchange, called Islamvision, was begun. This is a cooperative venture centering on Jeddah, Saudi Arabia which seeks common ground among islamic states of the Middle East but also includes Southeast Asia's Brunei, Indonesia and Malaysia. According to the RTM-Malaysia news director, the real intent of this service is to diffuse islamic fundamentalism by making available programming which shows the progressive side of islam.

In the Caribbean region, programme exchanges began in 1986. The Caribvision news exchange operates daily for about 45 minutes via Intelsat among the countries that host up and down-links (Barbados, Curacao, Jamaica and Trinidad) and intermittently among those with terrestrial interconnections. Using the Caribbean model, a group of African nations started trading television news in 1991. Afrivision is a daily exchange among nine mostly-north and west African states. Two different satellites are being used. The coordination centre is in Algeria.

Asiavision, Arabvision, Caribvision, Afrivision – and similar arrangements struggling to get going in Latin America and the South Pacific – are attempts to model the successes of Eurovision and similar news exchanges in the more developed world. Their motivation is to share locally-collected stories among neighbours and to pass on stories of international interest for broader consumption. It goes without saying that with daily exchanges among satellite partners, there are more opportunities for improving regional understanding, because of the greater depth and frequency in reporting, and the outward feeds help to counter the essentially one-way flow of news North to South.

Much credit is owed UNESCO for its assistance over many years and to the organizing work of the Broadcasting Unions (which UNESCO helped to establish) in each region. Financial and logistic support have been given by several international organizations based in the developed world interested in seeing that local news got more international visibility. The Frederich Ebert Foundation is one example. This German-based organization is helping the African states exchange get off the ground. Interestingly, personnel from the Caribbean Broadcasting Union have served as consultants on the Afrivision project and Caribbean-Africa exchanges are planned, a model for constructive South-South co-operation.

Regional news exchanges have both structural and content implications for the new information order journalism. The technologies of cross-border communication, made available through Intelsat and the regional satellite systems, have helped to put to the test traditional assumptions about periphery-to-centre relationships. For formerly news-dependent nations, the capability to collect and distribute their own news gives them a way to break out of the old order, making possible what has been so difficult to manage until now: horizontal exchanges between neighbouring or near-neighbouring states. It gives nations far from one another unprecedented opportunities to tell their own stories in their own way, in some cases by-passing the First World altogether.

The difference is not just the impact of 'glasnost' and democratization movements being felt around the world. The instruments of information production and distribution are more universally available. The cost, portability and easy maintenance of the new electronic news-gathering equipment, for example, are giving local news organizations the means to collect and edit news of sufficient quality to be acceptable for international distribution. Such technologies benefit agencies of state, who continually seek the means to extend the reach of their communications, but they have also permitted by-pass of the traditional gatekeepers, who by their authoritarian control or economic power have tended to restrict access to the limited number of information channels. Now, private and public, state and non-state broadcasters all are competing to get their news before the public.

Armenia, Estonia, Latvia and Lithuania by 1991 had each established independent relationships with CNN and were contributors to the *World Report*. It is noteworthy that the Soviet authorities were so afraid of a difference of opinion that, as the tanks once again rolled across the Lithuanian border in the last desperate year of the Soviet 'Union,' the troops went straight for the TV station. So strong was the resolve of the citizens of Vilnius to keep communication channels open that 16 died and 600 were wounded protecting that facility.

Robert Mavisakalian, editor in chief of Armenian state television, says of the *CNN World Report*, 'There are one million Armenians in the USA and two or three million elsewhere. We have no other way of getting them news of Armenia'. He explains with pride, 'If I may say so, Armenia is a very civilized country. We have 5000 years of history. In the fourth century Christianity was accepted as the state religion. But today people don't know where Armenia is much less know what is happening there. *World Report* is our only way out'.

Finland, Sweden and Iceland are prototypes of countries that in the past have not had the means to report for themselves. Rather, it fell their lot to be the dependent ones waiting to be reported upon. But from October 1987 through March 1992 Finland was able to get 155 of its stories aired on the CNN network via the weekly *World Report*, while Iceland aired 95 and Sweden 94. Each is now active in generating news for international distribution centering not only on the homeland but each goes out to cover events in other countries. Datelines for SVT-1 Sweden stories, with Malcolm Dixelius reporting, include Germany and Romania, Tanzania and Thailand, Albania and South Africa.

It is within this context the CNN-sponsored news exchange has emerged. *World Report* exchange is different from Eurovision, Asiavision, Caribvision and the others in that any country, in fact any public or private broadcast news organization with the resources to do so, has automoatic access to an internationally-distributed channel. CNN receives these stories via satellite (or by air freight) in Atlanta, packages each item into a two to three hour newscast and, serving as a kind of common carrier, delivers contributed stories back to participating news editors in almost every population centre in the world. CNN offers this service free of charge, encouraging editors to use the material on their local stations.

The structure is designed to insure that 'the many voices' of the world are heard. Reporters may cover crises and disasters, at home or abroad, or give background on stories of local interest. They may offer perspectives on world events, such as the changes taking place in Eastern Europe and in Africa, or join with others in examining issues of mutual concern, such as the state of the environment, the plight of refugees, or report domestic attitudes toward AIDS, or abortion, or religious intolerance. They may, if they like, use the exchange to engage in arguments and recriminations with their neighbours, or simply to promote local tourist attractions.[4]

Angola, Bulgaria and Vietnam are typical of the regular contributors to CNN's *World Report*. TPA-Angola has contributed 87 stories to the weekly programme, VTV-Vietnam has contributed 105 and BT-Bulgaria 186. BT-Bulgaria has contributed an additional 47 stories to the daily programme. Before Ted Turner gave Vietnam a satellite dish (in 1990) by which it could receive CNN from Intelsat directly, VTV-Vietnam got its CNN feeds by way of Moscow on Intersputnik. Vietnam's contributions, as are the contributions of Bulgaria, in 1992 were still relayed to Atlanta via Intersputnik.

CNN had to get special permission from the US Federal Communications Commission and the US State Department to take the Intersputnik signal. A local company, UPSouth in Atlanta, was under contract to track the Intersputnik Stationar 4, downlinking the daily news feeds of Intervision, including VREMYA, the influential state news programme of the former USSR.

Until 1992, CNN's international feeds were carried out on the Intersputnik satellite Stationar 12 which has a wide footprint reaching from Norway to South Africa, from the eastern edge of Brazil to Indonesia. Countries such as Tunisia, on the perimeter of the Intelsat 332 footprint, which the Turner organization uses to reach Europe, would get a clearer CNN signal from the Stationar 12.

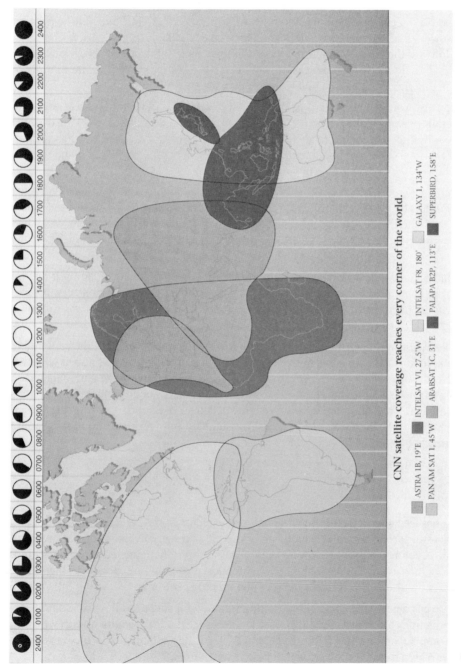

CNN satellite coverage reaches every corner of the world.

ASTRA 1B, 19°E   INTELSAT VI, 27.5°W   INTELSAT F8, 180°   GALAXY 1, 134°W

PAN AM SAT 1, 45°W   ARABSAT 1C, 31°E   PALAPA B2P, 113°E   SUPERBIRD, 158°E

CNN world satellite coverage map.

As a result of new agreements with the Arabsat, Astra, Galaxy, Intelstat, Palapa and PanAmSat organizations, CNN's signal now reaches most of the populated earth. The high-powered Astra 1B satellite at 19°East provides effective coverage of Western Europe. Arabsat 1C at 31° serves West Africa, the Middle East and India. The Indonesian Palapa B2-P at 113° reaches all of SE Asia, including Indonesia, Malaysia, the Philippines and New Zealand The wide footprint of Intelsat VA at 180° reaches the Eastern Commonwealth of Independent States and part of the Middle East and Africa. Galaxy V at 135° looks at the USA, Canada and the Caribbean. PanAmSat at 168° addresses South America. Local television broadcasters who contribute to *World Report* are eligible to downlink this signal and use as much of it as they like.

News has also been gathered into Atlanta on these satellites. 'Our more direct access to Intersputnik helped,' Libby Abbott, CNN senior satellite coordinator, explained in the Fall 1990. 'Earlier we got our feeds from Europe by way of London, fed to Atlanta along with the material sent from our bureau there. Now we can book directly out of the Eastern states'.

'We would never have dreamed of going up from Latvia. Not that the systems didn't exist but they didn't let you use them'. On Abbott's desk was an atlas in which she and others on the CNN satellite desk had been marking the places in the world from which they had been feeding visual news directly. Places like Vilnius in Lithuania and Donetsk in the USSR.

'Someone asked us, how do you feed from those regions? We had been doing it but we didn't even know how the connections were made. We had to ask our contacts. It turns out they were using landlines to Moscow. Before, often the only solution was to send a reporter in with a camera and fly the cassette out'.

Turner Broadcasting has five flyaway antennas – two 2.4 and three 1.8 metre portable satellite uplinks – to bring news in from the field. Each of the units is equipped with two sets of electronics so that, when necessary, two feeds can be transmitted simultaneously. Breaking stories from Prague, Bucarest and the Berlin wall were all brought in with a 1.8 metre antenna. This equipment, which was trucked into Baghdad during the Allied offensive in the Persian Gulf war, can be disassembled into 50 kilogram cases that are transported as air freight.[5]

Training

Training has also been a factor. Because of the new technologies, grassroots participation in broadcasting from rural and remote areas as well as the involvement of stations from the lesser-developed regions is now a practical possibility. Changing technologies require new skills, however. To meet this need, broadcast stations are devoting increasing attention to up-grading staff skills and regional training centres are attracting full classes.

Singapore has a new US$5.8 million training school with seven studios for radio/television production, broadcast journalism, dance and speech.[7] Instructors are drawn from Hong Kong, Japan and the BBC. Even small Nepal has established a media training centre with help from UNESCO, Japan, France and Norway.

One of the organizations that has worked hardest at helping Asia-Pacific countries develop its journalistic and news production skills has been the Asia-Pacific Broadcast Union (ABU). The ABU is the youngest of the international broadcasting groups, in the pattern of the European Broadcasting Union and Intervision. It is a private association with a mandate to assist in developing cooperative programmes in the region, to encourage the use of broadcasting for national development and to foster international understanding and good will through broadcasting activities.

The most important force for training in the Asia Pacific is the ABU's Institute of Broadcast Development. The AIBD, headquartered in Malaysia, is a regional broadcasting training centre for upgrading of broadcasting personnel and systems. Fifteen years old in 1992, it has provided training for some 10,000 participants from 38 countries within the region.

The purpose of the regional training centres is to assist member countries in improving their professional capabilities through training and research in broadcast management, programming and production, engineering and operations, news and current affairs and research and programme evaluation. A conscious effort is made to orient the work of broadcast organizations toward educational and development goals, and to create collaborative networks among participating nations.

CNN has its own training programme for *World Report* contributors. Three times a year CNN hosts a six-week internship at its facility in Atlanta, to provide 'education and first hand experience in production and coverage of world events'. The International Professional (IPP) programme, according to company literature, focuses on 'new journalistic and technical perspectives' and is designed to 'foster a more varied understanding of world issues'. IPP interns have come mostly from the developing world, countries such as the Cameroons, Czechoslovakia, Egypt and Ethiopia, but they have also come from China, Finland, Poland, Switzerland and the Soviet Union. Ten training sessions have now been completed, with delegates from more than 30 countries participating.

Cable TV and other outlets

The growing number of outlets using news material also has had an impact on *World Report*. Only when there are channels to carry such programmes can the amount and variety of TV news be increased. These channels are multiplying world-wide. Even in the United States some 4000 low power television stations have received licenses since 1982, when the FCC permitted translator stations to originate their own programming and began accepting applications for new LPTV stations. In the crowded media environment of the USA even a few additional full-power stations have also been approved.

As a result of privatizing of state-owned broadcast operations and joint venture financing of telecommunications within the newly industrialized countries of Latin America and Asia, and the opening of Eastern Europe, there is potential for much greater channel growth. According to the Center for Strategic and International Studies in Wasington D.C., during the mid-1990s more than 1000 new private television stations are projected to come on air in Western Europe alone.

Barbara Grad, foreign news editor for Polish TV, notes that applications are pending for 20 new regional television stations in Poland. In 1992 there are only two stations whose broadcast coverage is nationwide. 'If small power stations are approved, there will be many, 100 or more,' she said. 'This government – all governments – like to be the sole owner of the airwaves but the pressure of the society is so great'. She predicts the private broadcast stations will be approved.

Broadcast stations are, obviously, not the only options. With pressures on the electromagnetic spectrum from emerging communications technologies such as digital audio broadcasting, cellular radio, personal communications networks and high definition television, additional over-the-air stations will be harder and harder to find. The prime channels for TV broadcasting to the home, namely those using VHF and UHF frequencies, have for the most part already been allocated in regions where terrestrial broadcasting is economically and geographically feasible.[8] Thus, cable TV, wireless cable and direct to home broadcasting via satellite are emerging as viable alternatives.

Outside of the USA, except in a few places such as Belgium, cable is still undeveloped. Wiring of communities for cable distribution of programming to the home will, in fact, not happen everywhere because of the cost of laying and maintaining the cable and the dim prospects for financial return on investment. Some cities, such as Hong Kong and Singapore, have well-developed cable systems designed not just for video but to provide for their emerging 'information societies' linking videotex, facsimile and interactive terminals.

American regional telephone companies have been rather aggressively purusing the cable television business abroad. Along with Bell Atlantic, Ameritec now has a US$2.5 billion investment in New Zealand. With US West, Bell Atlantic is establishing a major presence in Czechoslovakia. US WEST, already a major player in UK cable, has recently signed big contracts with Hungary, and is making deals in Norway, Sweden, St. Petersburg (formerly Leningrad), Mexico and Latin America, and has ambitions in Asia. A big contract for installing cable in Yugoslavia was let to a Canadian company. A private cable corsortium, in collaboration with Polish TV and the Polish telecommunication authority, reportedly has approval to wire up the whole of Poland. At least two cities, Warsaw and Gdansk, are now wired for as many as 80 channels each.

Multipoint distribution service (MDS), more popularly called Wireless Cable, is a new option in direct to home broadcasting. Operating in the super high frequencies of the electromagnetic specturum, this service uses an omni-directional microwave transmitter to distribute an over-the-air signal in a broadcast pattern.[9] When cable cannot be laid for reasons of cost or for reasons of geography, wireless cable will sometimes be the alternative.

The advantage of wireless cable is that, unlike VHF and UHF-TV, multiple channels of high-quality audio and video can be transmitted from the same source. In the United States, where as many as 30 MDS channels are possible in each market, multichannel MDS is being used to distribute cable programming within cities not yet wired for cable. And, in a few locations, MMDS is being installed as a commercial competitor to cable systems already in place.

Viewers in Mexico City now have the opportunity to watch CNN via Multivision Stereo. Beginning in the Fall 1989, MVS's pay TV MMDS system began carrying CNN's 24 hour news service, which includes *World Report*. Prior to the agreement between Turner Program Services and MVS, CNN was only available in hotels and embassies in Mexico City. In 1990, AT&T International was the contractor in the construction of an MMDS station in Nairobi, Kenya and another was planned for Lagos, Nigeria. The Kenya station, an advertising-supported pay television service seen on Channel 62, carries CNN. This station is approved as a competitor to the government station.

Although not many countries have adopted the MMDS approach, it is an attractive option. The cost of constructing an MMDS system is much less than laying a cable system. MMDS can provide the additional channels needed without waiting for per- mission to lay cable along public streets and across private property. MMDS can be funded as a subscription service, in which viewers can choose to purchase all or a more limited number of channels, with the special receiving antennas provided as a part of the basic price.

Some cities may never be wired for cable TV for another reason: the impending deploy- ment of a different type services, direct to home satellite broadcasting. DBS is intended to by-pass the terrestrial broadcaster and cable programme distributor. Because of its unique vantage point from space, it can deliver a uniformly strong signal to those households within its footprint. Multiple channels of programming, 100 channels or more from a single service, are being talked about.

Although there is not yet a profitable DBS service in Europe, DBS development is probably as advanced there as any place. The United Kingdom, Germany, France, Scandanavia, Luxembourg and Italy all are struggling to bridge their social, cultural, political and economic differences so they can bring a direct to home satellite service that Europeans will embrace. With the announcement in May 1990 that the electronics giants Philips and Thompson were embarked on a US$3.6 billion venture to advance a Euro- pean HDTV standard to begin satellite broadcasting with the 1992 Barcelona Olympics, the pace of DBS development seems to be quickening.

Television programming is already being beamed to hotels and resorts, embassies and government offices and even to the back-yard satellite dishes of private citizens in most regions of the world. Almost all of this programming comes by way of low or medium power satellites and such transmissions require the larger more cumbersome and expens- ive receivers. With higher power satellites in the offing, smaller less expensive home reception equipment and abundant programme options to choose from, the window for news opens wider.

Consumer interest

Although hard data is lacking to back up the hypothesis, one reason we are seeing an increased interest in programmes such as *World Report* is that world viewers want more options in their television programming. Television audiences everywhere got a taste of what it means to have a choice. They want to see a greater variety of sporting events, more local programmes, more international programmes, more children's programmes, more movies, more news. And they want these programmes to be made available at more flexible hours, at times when they are free to sit down and watch.

'It used to be the public was absolutely indifferent to what is happening in the rest of the world,' says Szekly Ferenc, a journalist from Hungary, speaking of Eastern Europe in 1991. 'Now the people are more interested in neighbouring countries. Now they want to see what is happening in Czechoslovakia and Poland and, of course, the USSR. What is important is the Soviet Union and, indirectly, China. With the opening of China, the USSR has to fear the real competitor,' he explained. 'This is an important factor in our contributing to World Report'.

Having 24 hours of continuous news opens the market for a broader news agenda. When the six o'clock evening news is the only time the news is there to be viewed, only the universal items of most pressing priority are seen. The bringing down of the Berlin wall, Iraq's occupation of Kuwait, the breakup of the Soviet Union, and the whites-only referendum to end apartheid in South Africa are stories that may be the news everywhere, but clearly there is also an audience for much of the news that falls unused to the newsroom floor or is never collected for one reason or another. There is an audience for alternative perspectives on that news. TV critic David Gritten of the Los Angeles *Herald Examiner*, in applauding CNN's use of *World Report* to provide the news that networks ignore, says, 'It's hard to think of a time in the past decade when, because so much is happening in other parts of the world, American television viewers needed so much global perspective from the news they absorb'.[10]

A CNN audience study showing that 60 per cent of CNN viewers only stay tuned for five minutes or less at a time, says something about the 24-hour news service. The public tune in more often, to keep informed, but actively search out topics of most personal interest. CNN is indeed a 'fast food news service' but it also hosts more feature material, as in *World Report*. If, as described by a member of the regular CNN staff, 'the operating philosophy of CNN is to tell us what happened and to tell us in two minutes,' how will *World Report* material compete as CNN goes faster and faster, seeking harder, hotter and more timely news?

Ed Turner, CNN executive vice president, gives the official view. It doesn't have to compete. *World Report* is a unit within the news organization just as medicine, nutrition, science, sports and weather are units. Each makes its own contribution, each has its own pacing and each has its own appeal. Headline News has more hard news, it reports the news of the moment, there is less time for background and context. There is room for *World Report* in the mix.

Stuart Loory, former *World Report* editor-in-chief, echos this view. The departments of CNN, the news they present, should be viewed as different pages of a newspaper. The front page is for those who want the headlines and notice of the breaking events of the day. The op-ed page is for those who want opinion and perspective. *World Report* is more like the opinion and editorial page.

Loory says that *World Report* has given the lie to conventional wisdom about the American audience. Americans do have international interests, he says. They will put up with less than crisp audio and less than perfect pictures and will want more than

10-second sound bites when the content is compelling. Among American audiences, at least among those who watch *World Report*, the attention span appears not as short and the news interests not as narrow as we've all come to believe, Loory says.

Profitability

Another factor in the growth of the international news exchange is the money side. Rani Dilawari, a journalist from India who did an internship at CNN, found it ironic that an American commercial broadcaster would be using Third World journalists and seeking out their perspectives on world news. This had been a goal of UNESCO's New World Information and Communication Order, to reduce Western domination of international news flow and news opinion, but the news-dependent nations were looking in the direction of government to make some change in this situation. She attributed CNN's move to cultivating Third World journalists to the economics of competing in an international news arena.

'CNN, being primarily a news organization, had to find continuous sources of news with the least financial investment. Only a programme like the *World Report* could provide an answer to the CNN's increasing need for television news sources in every part of the world,' she said.

The 'unedited/uncensored' principle was what the developing countries had been looking for to tell their side of the story to the West, Dilawari concluded. The *World Report* instantly made CNN the clearing house for a diversity of news stories that no other station could have even if it spent a fortune. It also made *World Report* a carrier of certain types of stories nobody else would have wanted. Many of the *World Report* stories would never have been picked up by any other service, either because they were too provincial, too self-promotional or just poorly done.

The Turner organization did run a risk. When in the late 1980s Ted Turner announced his goal to make CNN the first private company broadcasting to the whole world, there were those in the developing world who distrusted the programme and its intentions. Here was another American media venture out to spread American culture. CNN's international newscast would make money but at the expense of the Third World.

Sohair Hafez, news reporter for ETV-Egypt, was very frank in saying, 'At first we thought 'It's too good to be true'. We had second thoughts about it but eventually went ahead to try it'. By early 1992, the weekend *World Report* had aired 76 stories originating with Egyptian Television with 13 of its contributions appearing on the daily *World Report*. Still, in making use of the *CNN World Report* material in Egypt, she said there are 'lingering doubts about the venture coming from the United States'.

Now it appears that Turner will not be without competition. Japan's public broadcaster NHK announced at the 1991 National Association of Broadcasters convention in Las Vegas that it was initiating a US\$1 billion 24-hour Global News Network (GNN) which would debut 'within the year' as a partnership of NHK and certain (unnamed) European and US broadcasters.[11] As of 1992 the GNN service had apparently faltered but the BBC had inaugurated an entirely new 24-hour visual news service called World Service

Television, which it was testing in Asia using the new Asiasat satellite and which, it says, is a first step toward world-wide delivery, including delivery in the United States. Rupert Murdoch's Sky News Channel, operating as a satellite delivered service over Europe and North Africa, is generally expected to expand its global presence.

What is not so easy to understand or for the staff to explain is that the *World Report* is an expense, not a source of income for the Turner organization. While *CNN World Report* does not pay its contributors, neither can it charge for the retransmission and further use of that news. And the personnel commitment and satellite and shipping costs of hosting the exchange are enormous.

'Believe me,' Stuart Loory told contributors in 1989, 'the *CNN World Report* costs CNN a lot of money'. He reminded them, 'We started this programme with two people – Brooke McDonald and myself – and the feeling was that production could be done in another part of the house as an add-on duty, with no increase in facilities or charges of any kind. When we were a twenty-eight report programme – just getting started and nobody was paying any attention to us – that worked. For about three weeks. Then we began adding facilities, people, computers, networks of customs brokers, telexes and every-thing. 'Our telex bill these days – I shouldn't say telex any longer because of the fax revolution – but our communications bill now runs upwards of US$10,000 a month, just keeping in touch with all of you'.

The *CNN World Report*, Loory explained, does carry advertising but it is advertising that is sold generically and placed throughout the programming every day of the week. 'That revenue covers the normal kind of programming. It does not cover the kind of thing in which we spend now four or five thousand dollars a week to mail tapes out to you, those of you who cannot receive the programme by satellite'.

'We have been doing *CNN World Report* with mirrors. It is a grand concept but it is a concept for which we started with no budget,' he said. 'We now have a budget that we can certainly live with and we are not complaining about it in any way, but believe me, it is not an elaborate budget and it is not one that allows us to go out, for example, and book a weekly satellite'.

He tried to reassure contributors, 'We are not making money on the sweat of your brow, or the largesse of the treasuries of your organizations, or the money you are laying out. We feel that the arrangement we have – you provide us with three minutes once a week, as infrequently as once a month and we provide you with three or more hours worth of programming a week – is a pretty good deal. We think it's a good deal for us, and at least as good a deal for all of you'. Loory got very little disagreement from his audience.

Stuart Purvis, editor of Independent Television News, writing in *The Listener*[12] admitted he had been skeptical but concluded *World Report* was another 'Ted Turner classic: a genuine wish to use television to improve international understanding, combined with a shrewd business and public relations strategy'. This strategy, identified by Purvis and others, appears to be based on three principles: to invest up-front in an international newscast that will create an appetite and a market for CNN news services, to develop close journalistic ties with news organizations throughout the world and to gain access to valuable archival footage from all corners of the globe.

To this point, the pundits appear to be correct. Turner can 'do good' and at the same time build an international base for his news organization. CNN was the first American network to sell its programmes to the Soviet Union. TSS-Soviet Union was an active contributor from the very first programme. The International Hour, in which the daily *World Report* appears, is reported to be a good selling point for CNN marketers who are trying to get CNN service placed on international services. And back home, *World Report* footage adds visual impact, timeliness and credibility to CNN reporting on international events.

World Report has its own daily and week-end slots, but some of this news is picked up for use by other departments of CNN. From ETV-Ethiopia, CNN got its pictures of the plane crash that led to the death of US congressman, Mickey Leland. It got its first story on the Iraqi invasion of Kuwait from Egyptian television. Mjusa Sever of TV Libra-Yugoslavia gave CNN viewers their first glimpse of what was happening in Romania. Sever was also reporting on the tensions between Serbs and Croats months before the blow-up of ethnic rivalries in Yugoslavia. According to the *World Report* staff, for the first few days into the violence in Yugoslavia, the network relied almost entirely on stories filed by *World Report* contributors.

'As a global network, (the *World Report*) serves a number of purposes,' says Eason Jordan, international managing editor for CNN. 'From the news side, it is outstanding in opening doors'. He gave as an example CNN's coverage of the release of Nelson Mandela. The South African government had hedged on providing CNN live coverage but were eventually persuaded. He attributes the breakthrough to help given by *World Report* contacts at SABC. A similar situation occurred at the time of the assasination of Rajiv Gandhi, he said. 'It helps if they already know who you are'.

The next generation of foreign correspondents for the US media, says Scott Shuster writing in the *Columbia Journalism Review*, may be foreign. Shuster's argument is that the local reporter is already in place and will cost a tenth of what is needed to maintain an American in the field. What is more important, the native already has a visa, doesn't need a translator and is familiar with the territory.

'As competitors,' he says, 'these European and third world journalists are terrifying. They routinely work in two or three languages. They know their beats as well as you know your hometown because their beat frequently is their hometown. American reporters can sputter all they like about the importance of being a foreign observer, the necessity of knowing the audience back home, the need for an American accent in broadcast presentation – that's just a lot of protectionist babble. The truth is all that stuff can be learned. There is an army of foreign journalists out there, ready to put an end to the ancient and ridiculous practice of sending speak-only-English American reporters half-way around the world to pretend to be experts on places they have never seen before'.[13]

At the first conference of contributors in Atlanta, which included some 200 TV broadcast people from almost a hundred countries, Ed Turner, the CNN vice president, showed a videotape explaining that 'While the other older US broadcast organizations are retrenching, CNN is opening six new international bureaus: Seoul, Manila, Athens, Geneva, Brussels and Madrid. We are doubling the size of our Moscow bureau this year, adding another correspondent, crew and field producer ... . Since we have 24 hours to fill our reports cover the positive stories in those coutries, as well as the stories reflecting upheaval. We have the time and the interest for the good, as well as the bad'.

Ed Turner let participants know that it was CNN's desire to make as much use of the *World Report* contributions in the regular newscast as possible. Part of the job of the staff is to see to it that those materials are not overlooked, that the International Desk is kept apprised of hard news leads, or of events that have changed. 'Where a *World Report* piece might not be too current, all of a sudden because of changes in the country, it has interest again,' he said. 'Or there's a story broken in country *x* that gives this story in country *y* a currency, a certain urgency that it didn't have before'.

He credited *World Report* staff for looking out for network interests. 'When they have pieces come in, a piece in hand, or know of a piece headed for a bureau that they know is perishable and has high value as a spot news piece,' he said, 'they're very quick to alert all of us about it. They look out after their show,' he noted, 'but they look out for the network as well'.

International politics

Politics also figure as a factor in the emergence of *World Report*. In the unpredictable melee of modern events, governments are losing their grip on the news. Border walls are being brought down by political dissent and demands for economic restructuring; government media are being by-passed by those with access to competing technology. Competition is being introduced to government-controlled monopolies. The national services are increasingly deregulated, decentralized, democratized or just no longer in control. Outgroups have greater access to the communication equipment, giving them unprecedented opportunity to speak for their own causes and constituencies. Joint media ventures and co-productions set the stage for cooperative programming among nations. Development organizations, fund raisers and religious organizations have begun to use the international airways to reach wider audiences. The English language has been made more central to information sharing. The public, especially in the news starved regions of the world, is wanting more access to what is going on.

In a remarkable session of a *World Report* contributors conference hosted by CNN, journalists talked about the role TV news played in the break-up of the Eastern Bloc. Dr. Andrzej Drawcz, president of Polish TV, told the assembled broadcasters how proud he was when Reuters cited Polish TV as a source. 'I always have that telex on my desk to comfort me in difficult moments. A proof of success, however modest it was,' he said. It was a point of pride for him when Polish TV was no longer seen by others as a mouthpiece of the state. It was a noteworthy accomplishment when his reporters were viewed as professionals capable of deciding for themselves what is important to report and sufficiently independent of the state to handle stories objectively.

Eugen Freund, foreign desk reporter for ORF-Austria, told of the thrill of showing the news pictures of May 1989, when the Hungarian and Austrian ministers cut through the wire fence separating their countries signaling the end of the border guards and the bitter language of fear and recrimination. He told of his amazement in seeing the tearing down of the Berlin wall leading to the re-unification of Eastern and Western Germany, and the opening of Czechoslovakia. In his view, TV news had a hand in this. TV helped to push along movements that had already begun. Along their western borders the people of Hungary, Czechoslovakia and Yugoslavia could get Austrian television. Due to TV, those people were already aware of the differences in lifestyle with the West. They were able to compare and their discontent was evident.

When the Soviet paratroopers took over the buildings of his city, Algimantas Jokubenas of Lithuania told how the people came to defend the TV station. Television had been important in the Lithuanian independence movement, he said. Reporters were free to report what they liked and journalists were permitted to express their own thoughts. He described a popular public call-in programme called *Mirror* on Lithuanian TV. 'It was the first programme in the Soviet Bloc to criticize the government,' he said.

Peter Popescu of TRL-Romania described how he took the floor upon his appointment as Public Relations Director of the national television service and apologized to the people for the lies that had been told. He made a public commitment on behalf of the television organization to tell the truth. 'TV is the highway to revolution in our country, because everyone looks at TV,' he said. 'It is from TV they get their information'. He quoted from one of Aesop's fables which says words can be the gentlest thing in the world, but words can kill. 'Television is the same, this invention of our time, of our day. It can do great good for our people, but it can also do a lot of damage'.

Eduard Sagalayev, VREMYA editor, quoted Marx. 'The most unassailable fortress in the world is the human skull,' he told the delegates assembled at CNN. 'It is television which is the weapon which can penetrate it. And if that is taking place, then all of the other barriers fall down, as was the case with the Berlin wall'. When Soviet TV began showing in graphic detail the events in East Germany, in Czechoslovakia and in Romania, 'there was a very sharp stepping up of political activity in the most varied places and localities of our enormous country. There was a chain of what we would call province revolutions'.

'Fortunately, at the time of the collapse of the old regimes of Eastern Europe, reforms in our country had already advanced sufficiently and gone far enough so that our military and our rightist politicians were not tempted to introduce Soviet tanks into those countries. Indeed, quite the opposite'. Sagaleyev credited Soviet TV with this feat and noted in fact the way TV 'served to attone for that guilt which we feel towards mankind for the events of 1956 and 1968 and several other cataclysms which are well-known to everybody'.

Now with the transitions occuring in the Commonwealth of Independent States (CIS), all freely covered by the newsmedia, the trend of movement is toward greater pluralism and local empowerment in communication. In Eastern and Central Europe, as elsewhere, alternatives are being sought to government-owned and government-controlled media. In 1990 the Zambian government sent Dr. Steven Moyo, director general of the Zambian National Broadcasting Corporation, to CNN to learn how to run the government channel as a private station.

'This is a very radical departure when you know that in the Third World – and in our part of the world specifically – the media has tended to be controlled by the government in power,' says Moyo. 'The (ZNBC), as of now, does not openly receive government financing. What is happening, in fact, is that we are fending for ourselves and this money is coming mainly from advertising and programme underwriting. The government, like everybody else, pays for the services it receives'.

Labour unions, religious groups, political organizations, business and industrial organizations are finding ways to by-pass the traditional monopolies of the state to tell their stories and interact with others. These groups have begun to rely on their own resources, trust their own abilities to define problems as they see them, set goals, devise strategies and make decisions independent of those officially in charge.

News is also being deinstitutionalized. Not only are the alternative media springing up, in some cases visual news is being received directly from people in the streets who have their own cameras. Common people, untrained as journalists or as videographers, are getting encouragement from stations to cover and offer for airing events they think newsworthy. CNN advertises a 'news hound' option. Near the end of the Persian Gulf crisis, CNN was giving small hand-held cameras to Kurdish refugees making their way back to Iraq. The refugees were allowed to keep the cameras but were asked to take pictures of what they saw and to try to get the tapes back. In these instances, the traditional gatekeeper roles are relaxed, the public is more in a position to contribute, the stories are less predictable.

International news has also gotten involved in international relations, even in international negotiations. Because they have access to the same world news, heads of state often know the reactions of other world leaders before they hear from them personally. A classic example of this was described by Can Dundar of the TRT-Turkey foreign news department. Turkey's president Ozal, at the time of the Iraqi invasion, was watching CNN coverage of the press conference of US president Bush from Kennebunkport, Maine. In response to a question, Bush told a reporter that the first thing he was going to do as soon as the press conference was over was to call President Ozal. According to Dundar, Ozal got up from his chair and walked into the next room. The phone rang. It was President Bush.

One year later, at the time of the attempted coup in the USSR, President Bush had cut short his vacation in Kennebunkport. In his first press conference from Washington, a reporter asked the President if he had been in touch with President Gorbachev, who was assumed to be under house arrest in the Crimea. 'We have tried,' he said, 'but we have not been successful'. Another reporter asked if it wasn't likely that Gorbachev was at this very moment watching his press conference? 'Yes, it's very likely,' he said.

'East and West have become truely linked,' says Selina Chow, chief executive officer of ATL-Hong Kong. 'The impact and effect of major events are now experienced on a global scale. The happenings and the reporting of them to the rest of the world are now inseparable'. In her opinion, 'Deliberate efforts to hide the truth are becoming more difficult and, with the strengthening of international news networks, less likely to succeed'.

Chow says, because of television, the power of the people is more recognized and conceded to than ever before. She points to the toppling of the Marcos government, the democratization process in Taiwan, the student movement in Korea, the elections and independence movements which occurred in the Soviet Union and the allegations and charges of corruption among influential politicians in Japan, powerfully portrayed on television, as having 'inspired, stimulated, shaped views and changed attitudes of the audience, wherever and whoever they may be'.

The idea of a newscast consisting of international perspectives, such as the one made available through CNN's *World Report*, comes at a time when the international viewing audience is as open as it has ever been to hearing the other side. Even if the report is one-sided, so long as it is not the only view available, viewers seem to want to hear it. The background for the change is simple. There is enough doubt among viewers around the world that they are getting the complete picture from established sources they are willing to question the officially presented view – to question the facts as well as the interpretation and be open to alternatives. To come to their own conclusions, they need to know what the established reporters overlooked or failed to tell them.

Even in Vietnam, where the television is on only two and a half hours a day, from 6 to 9:30 p.m., and the news is only 20 minutes, the public is eager to get the news. According to the director general of Vietnam TV, Pham Khac Lam, 'The people in Vietnam want to see international news, the news they cannot see with their own eyes'. Lam is hoping in the near future to be able to increase the news slot to 45 minutes so more international news, such as that available on *CNN World Report*, can be made available to Vietnamese viewers. He also hopes the rest of the world will be open to hearing from Vietnam.

Public diplomacy

There are few nations which do not feel a need to project a particular image of themselves, to explain and promote their agendas to the rest of the world. Especially, in a time of great political upheaval and economic scrambling, the news is not a matter to be left to chance coverage by the international news agencies. Policy must be clarified, events updated, rumors corrected. *World Report* emerges at a time when nations are reaching out, using the media to present a new face and gain status in the rest of the world, to overcome stereotypes and misrepresentations of their countries or to make some appeal or present a point of view.

A 1990 news item prepared by Al Gurnov, TSS-Soviet Union correspondent, illustrates this. Gurnov's report was a story about the territories of the USSR, a kind of geography lesson for international viewers. People around the world know the small countries of Europe and the states of the United States, but not everybody knows about the states of the USSR. TSS thought it would be good way to help the international audience get a more complete picture of the country they were seeing so much about on TV.

Similarly, Aleksey Denisov, an early participant in the International Professional (IPP) training programme at CNN, produced a story for *World Report*, also shown on Soviet TV, of Soviet reaction to demolition of the East Berlin wall. 'We appreciate the opportunity to show to the American audience our point of view,' he said. 'We sometimes go even further than American journalists in covering events which criticize our country'. He pointed to the TSS story showing mothers crying on the graves of their dead children in the cemeteries of the USSR after the Afghanistan tragedy.

At the close of 1990, *CNN World Report* staff sent out a call for retrospectives, news stories prepared by contributors looking backward at the important events of 1990. BT-Bulgaria reported on a year of firsts for Bulgarians, the first free democratic elections, the first non-communist president and government and the first free and official celebration of Christmas. CCTV looked at China's world standing as a result of the boost given by the 1990 Asian games. It also noted for world viewers the lifting of martial law, new economic initiatives and its view that a new nation-wide concensus had emerged in China.

Some of the broadcasters making weekly contributions to *World Report* are government broadcasters with a public diplomacy mission, such as the mission served abroad by Voice of America and Worldnet of the US state department. Their mandate is to explain the policies of the government and convey to viewers abroad a more complete picture of life in the country from the point of view of that country. In fact, one way to view CNN's *World Report*, says Tommy Mandigora, news director for Zimbabwe Broadcasting Corporation, is as external broadcasting.

'Just like any other broadcasting station, an external service's basic objectives must be to inform, educate, and entertain listeners,' says Mandigora, 'to assist foreign listeners to understand the culture of the people of the host country (and) to inform the world on the views of the people and the policies of the governments of those countries. A deliberate effort must be made to highlight developments at home because they are often misrepresented by some sections of the foreign media'.

Mandigora also says developing countries must use such opportunities as the *World Report* presents to highlight their socio-economic and political achievements. 'Under the present world information order,' he says, 'achievements of developing countries are often ignored or underplayed by some transnational news agencies'.

Deutsche Welle, chartered to provide overseas broadcasting services for the Federal Republic of Germany, broadcasts by radio in 34 languages on a daily basis. In addition, it produces TV programmes for North America as well as the countries of Asia, Africa and Latin America. Deutsche Welle is a regular contributor to *World Report*. A recent DW-TV report looked at the number of Romanian refugees pouring across the border between Germany and Poland and the new German immigration law which makes it easier for Germany to deport illegal immigrants. Deutsche Welle, in a *World Report* story which preceeded the G-7 meeting in London, explained that Germany had already pledged US$35 billion in financial assistance to the Soviet Union and expected the other members of the seven largest industrialized nations to share the burden.

The goal of Germany's overseas broadcasting service, according to Siegfried Berndt, director of television for Deutsche Welle, is to provide programmes that are 'accurate, truthful and objective; they should promote the free international flow of information; and they should, above all, give the listeners living in a dictatorship, or in countries where the media are controlled or influenced by the state, the possibility to receive objective information on world affairs'.

Turner unorthodoxy

An international journalist asked Ted Turner from the floor at a contributor conference in Atlanta, 'I wonder if you could consider helping Third World countries by supplying – through a foundation possibly – these countries that would really like to do a better job in the *World Report*, with equipment to do a better job?'

Turner replied, 'well, we'd love to do that too. I'd like to see everybody supplied with everything, but we just don't have the money. I gave Vietnam a satellite receiver, but I did that because I felt guilty, not because of anything I personally did, but because of my nation picking on them for so long ... . What country are you from? Have we done anything bad to you?'

'My name is Ric Wasserman from Angolan Television,' the man responded. Turner answered, 'I'll tell you what. You know, you've got these little hand-held cameras now that cost about a thousand dollars, and they work too. We get News Hound stories all the time on those hand-held cameras. Have you got one of them?' Wasserman said, 'No, can I pick it up?' Turner answered, 'Well, talk to Loory about it. I might be able to do it. But you understand, I'd love to do it. If I had all the money in the world, I'd do it'.

Enrico Woolford, Guyana TV, stood up. 'I'm not going to ask for anything. I was just wondering if perchance, as a media person, you were thinking of investing in other media in other parts of the world, perhaps in the way that Rupert Murdoch has done. Has that thought ever crossed your mind?'

'It's the same problem again,' Turner told him. I owe a billion and a half right now. I've already got debts that are greater than some Third World countries. I just don't have the money. I'd love to invest. I tried to invest with the Soviets. We were going to build some car washes in the Soviet Union, but we didn't have any money to build them with. It was a great idea, I could make a fortune ... . Look what I've done with no money. If I had some money, I'd be dangerous, but I don't have it. Maybe we could chip in with the Third World and come up with ... . I'm buying dinner, though. I'm buying lunch. That's about all I have enough money to do'.

This is typical Turner, playing the role of international diplomat and communicator, empathetic, optimistic, but always unpredictable. Many look to his leadership and he fits comfortably into the leadership role. 'Someone's got to be out there leading,' he said in 1990. 'In television, you can lead. You can initiate things.'[15]

One of his most persistent initiatives has been to try to create ways to reduce political tensions around the world and to improve the quality of the environment. According to former US president Jimmy Carter, Turner has contributed literally millions of dollars from his own pocket in support of the Better World Society, an organization that seeks to use television to advance a global agenda, specifically the 'survival issues' that could threaten the safety, security, viability of the planet: the arms race, the need for sustainable development and exponential population growth.

Tom Belford, Better World Society executive director, in addressing a group of international journalists presided over by Turner, explained the goals of the organization. 'Some of you use TV very deliberately to transmit national purpose, to share moral values, to educate and even engage in social marketing campaigns in things like health care, family planning and so forth. And for others, the emphasis is on the elusive concept of objectivity'.

'From our standpoint, the key question – the one that we ask ourselves as we approach using television, that we ask you to ask yourselves – is simply should we use the power of TV as an agent of change or to protect the status quo? For us, it's a fairly easy question to answer because as we see it, if you use television to serve or reinforce the status quo, you're condoning the arms race, you're condoning global degradation of the environment, you're permitting unsustainable population growth, you're accepting endless inhuman poverty for most people on this earth'. Belford pointed out, 'You answer it first and foremost by deciding what to cover and what not to cover'.

This is what is unorthodox about Ted Turner as a commercial broadcaster. Money is not all that is important. Turner is comfortable with using media as a source of good. Better when he can make doing good pay but clearly his preferences are to use media to the end of helping save the environment, in consciously promoting international understanding, in working for international peace, in looking for common ground. These personal goals translate into programmes. In the case of *World Report*, it translates into helping the less developed world get its message across and to help the rest of the world recognize that there can be more than one point of view.

Turner's excitement about his project comes through. 'I mean to tell ya, there's a whole world out there,' he says, 'and on the *World Report*, you see it in all its diversity'.

References

1. Don M. Flournoy, *Telecommunications in Asia*, Asia and the Pacific: Handbooks to the Modern World, London: Facts on file Publications, 1990.
2. *Ibid.*
3. Don M. Flournoy, 'Satellites in the National Interest,' *Satellite Communications*, February 1986.
4. Don M. Flournoy, 'International News Flow Surges into the 1990s,' *Media Development*, vol xxxvii/4, 1990.
5. Don M. Flournoy, 'Distribution of CNN's *World Report*,' *Satellite Communications*, February 1991.
6. Don M. Flournoy, 'Distribution Systems,' in Alan Richardson ed., *Corporate Video*, New York, McGraw-Hill, 1992.
7. *Op.cit.*, 'Telecommunications in Asia'
8. Don M. Flournoy and Misha Nedeljkovich, *Alternative Radio and Television Technologies, Radio and Television: Theory and Practice*, Belgrade, Yugoslavia, Winter, 1990.
9. *Ibid.*
10. David Gritten, 'TV's Two Windows on the World,' *Los Angeles Herald Examiner*, May 31, 1989.
11. 'NHK to Go Head-to-head with CNN,' *Broadcasting*, April 22, 1991.
12. Stuart Purvis, 'News of the World,' *The Listener*, May 22, 1989.
13. Scott Shuster, 'Foreign Competition Hits the News,' *Columbia Journalism Review*, May/June 1988.
14. Hank Whittemore, *CNN: The Inside Story*, Boston: Little, Brown and Company, 1990.
15. John Motavalli, 'Circle the wagons, Here Comes Ted Turner,' *Pinnacle*, September-October 1990.

Chapter 5   HOW TV NEWS ORGANIZATIONS SEE *WORLD REPORT*

'What CNN has done is instead of talking about changing television news, they have actually done something'
Steve Whitehouse, Anchor/Producer, United Nations Television

There is no doubt that with 185 broadcast organizations from 130 countries contributing news, at least half of whom contribute regularly, CNN has managed to assemble an international news network unlike any that has ever existed. Participants in this global newscast and international news exchange include the well-established players, such as the BBC and ITN of the United Kingdom, and those lesser-known such as BOP-TV of Boputaswana, South Africa, TCS News of El Salvador and BT-Bulgaria. Why do such organizations wish to affiliate with CNN?

Why are stations in Angola and Brazil and Czechoslovakia and Cyprus going to the trouble of preparing stories each week and transmitting them at their own expense to the United States without expectation of being paid for the effort? That is a question researchers at Ohio University asked.

In cooperation with CNN, *World Report* contributors were surveyed in 1989 and again in 1990 and 1991, to find out what types of news organizations participated in the exchange and learn their reasons for participating. An attempt was also made to understand the criteria the participating stations used in deciding what news to send to Atlanta. Questions were asked about any difficulties encountered and their assessment of how the exchange was working. Sixty nine news organizations from 63 nations and two international institutions (UNTV and Globalvision) responded. Forty one were from 'developing' countries; 26 were from 'developed' countries. Several responding organizations were not at the time of the survey active contributors but have now become so. Additional organizations were selected for in-depth interviews.

Global audience

American Samoa gave a somewhat typical response. 'We participate in CNNWR for two reasons. The main reason is to give our staff a chance to learn and better understand the rules and procedures of good reporting and editing in 'the big time'. Our second reason is to bring some news of 'home' to Samoans living in the United States and New Zealand. There are more American Samoans living abroad than here in the Samoan Islands. This also doesn't hurt our desire to better promote Samoa to a world who, for the most part, hasn't the slightest idea of who or where we are'.

A story submitted by KVZK-TV American Samoa during the time of the war in the Persian Gulf showed their people praying for the 7000 Samoans serving in the US military. From the news item *CNN World Report* viewers learned that American Samoa sends more soldiers into the US military than does any place else in the USA. Another story from this time period showed the broad public support among Samoans for President Bush and the Allied Forces in the Gulf.

The response given by the station manager of Discovery Television, Grenada, West Indies, was similar. 'We consider CNN a highly respected network. To be able to contribute stories of interest gives us a bit of their credibility. It also gives our Grenadian staff another opportunity to have their work showcased outside of Grenada ... filling a need to inform peoples of all cultures. In Grenada's case, while we have 113 thousand Grenadians living at home, more than 700 thousand Grenadians are living in England, Canada and the United States. It gives them a chance to know what's going on at home'.

Discovery Television is now off the air. It was a privately-owned station whose news reports to CNN were all especially-prepared for the *World Report* programme. That is, the reports were not taken from its regular newscasts. Based on an informal analysis of Discovery's contributions to the exchange, what was 'going on at home' that the station felt moved to communicate was Grenada's slow but steady recovery after the US invasion and its progress toward democracy. The station also reported on Grenada's efforts, in cooperation with those of its democratic neighbours, to interdict drug trafficking in the area.

Guyana, a neighbour in the Caribbean, doesn't use any of the incoming *CNN World Report* material even though it has contributed about 50 stories to CNN for airing on the weekend programme. Enrico Woolford, head of public affairs for Guyana Broadcasting and video producer, apologizes and explains that on the two private broadcast stations in Guyana there is only 10 minutes of news per day and only a limited audience is receiving that. Outside the cities there is no electricity or the electricity is out. 'GTV contributes to *CNN World Report* because we feel that not enough is known about current affairs in Guyana. Guyanese abroad need to know what's happening in their country'.

It is too simplistic to say that the main-line stations in West Germany, ARD, ZDF and Deutsche Welle, became contributors because of public pressure but it appears this was a motivating reason. At the time of the inauguration of the *World Report* service, CNN approached the German broadcasters but they weren't interested. Eureka TV, a private cablecaster, was the only one to take CNN up on its offer to cover the news from the German perspective.

Mary Amthor, an American married to a German, was hired by Eureka to produce stories for the CNN newscast. During the first year she sent in a programme every two or three weeks, about 15 submissions in all. She said she covered news events that were feasible to do, stories that were accessible to her: Octoberfest, a profile of Franz Joseph Straus, a tax reform bill, whatever was current and a little controversial. She tried to stay away from stereotypical Germany.

'My bosses wouldn't have let me present Germany in a negative light. There wasn't that much bad to report on anyway. The Olympics, a flashback, was somewhat negative. I just wanted to present an interesting story,' she said.

Amthor's pieces were 3:15 minutes in length or 3:20 or 4:00, never 3:00, she said. This means she counted on the *World Report* staff to either accept the piece as it was produced or to use their own discretion in cutting it to the requisite three minutes. Her video cassettes were sent by plane on Thursdays so that associate producer Brooke McDonald would receive them by Friday. Fortunately, Delta Airlines had a direct flight to Atlanta. Eureka paid about DM200 for this service. Nothing was ever sent by satellite.

Timeliness of the stories was often a problem. Amthor felt she couldn't do stories that were burning hot. She used old Octoberfest footage so she could prepare and send in the story before the event took place; she did the same with the tax debate story. Also, she felt she had to do a slightly different kind of story for the American audience. 'You have to tell the story to others differently because they are without the background. The assumptions are different. You have to bring it down to the clearest simplest level without being paternalistic. And you have to re-write the *CNN World Report* stories for the Germans'.

Germany's weekly magazine, *Gong*, in March 1988, raised the question publicly as to why ARD and ZDF turned down CNN's offer to send in reports. 'Even the German Democratic Republic (communist East Germany) took this opportunity,' wrote columnist Helmut Markwort. 'The most important stations in the world are invited to send in reports. More than 80 countries participate, from Japan to England to the Soviet Union ... . Why are ARD and ZDF so arrogant?' he asked.

'And now the hardly seen, not very professional private broadcaster, Eureka TV, supplies the portrait of Germany. What Eureka shows is better than nothing at all, but that in no way justifies the arrogance of both our giant networks that are financed with our money. Nor does it justify their ignorance. While intelligent people have been wracking their brains for years trying to figure out how they can improve, through film, Germany's appearance and reputation in the world, ARD and ZDF have arrogantly messed up their chance to do just this'.[1]

It turns out Eureka had difficulty sustaining its participation in the CNN programme. Its contributions were irregular and it found it almost never used the *World Report* material made available. According to Amthor, Eureka couldn't receive the satellite signals at its studios in Munich because a building blocked its view of the satellite. Later the company moved, enabling it to receive the signal but, because the CNN transmission came at an inconvenient time (6–8 a.m.), nobody wanted to go to the office early and tape it off the air. In any case, the news staff was unwilling to take the time to sit down and watch two hours of *CNN World Report* news when, in their opinion, the international news they were getting from World Television News and Visnews was more than enough.

During this time, Eureka started a new programme called the German report, which had some *World Report* material in it, translated. Usually the original reporters were cut out and the credits deleted. Sometimes just the pictures were pulled off and a new story written. Amthor recalled that pictures from a story on Angola and one about Mickey Mouse in China were used in this way. On the rare occasion that a *World Report* story was used in full it would have been a story originating from another European contributor with a European theme, she said.

A year later when Cologn, Berlin and Frankfurt began making regular submissions, as many as two or three stories a week were arriving in Atlanta from Germany, competing with each other to get on. Mary Amthor said she found herself calling up the other agencies to avoid using the same theme. Soon afterward Eureka was bought out, its mission changed and Amthor moved to Frankfurt and took a job with World Television News.

BT-Bulgaria and MOVI-Hungary both say they are participants because there is 'a possiblity to be seen internationally'. At home, 'a few thousand people will see what we produce, but on CNN the audience will be a few million'. Even though their use of *World Report* material is modest, 'The reports of CNN give us the possibility to show countries from where visual information can rarely be seen'.

The director general of Ethiopian TV explained, 'We participate in the CNNWR to show to the world in our own way what we are doing and what is happening in our country. We also participate to have access to other countries' reports from themselves, not from any third party. We believe it is the only forum to date where countries are provided with the unique opportunity of informing other peoples without any distortion'.

News exchange

It appears there are both altruistic and self-interest reasons for joining in the exchange. Twenty eight of the local broadcasters responding to the survey expressed interest in supporting a more equitable global exchange of television news, especially in seeing more Third World news being made available, and in promoting international understanding through greater competition and alternative sources in international news flow. Thirty seven of the stations noted their interest in publicizing life in their countries. They want to reach a wider audience, the American audience in particular, and they want to communicate news of home to those abroad. Of somewhat lesser importance was access to the programming of others. Not many, at least not at the time of the surveys, felt they could really use much of the *World Report* material. They did appreciate seeing how others handled news stories and thought that participating in the exchange was a good way to help develop professionalism within the news staff and build up the local news organization.

SVT-Sweden gave a rather surprising reason for participating. The station wishes to make contacts through the news exchange with countries where it doesn't have a regular contact, where it doesn't have its own correspondents. SVT hosts a globe-trotting news crew bringing stories back to the home audience and airing these on CNN's *World Report*. Of the 94 stories provided CNN, one half or more were not stories from a Swedish dateline but were stories collected and sent in by SVT crews working beats in other parts of the world. For *CNN World Report*, SVT has contributed stories from places as distant as Albania, Romania, Siberia, Thailand, Tanzania and South Africa.

TV Manchete of Brazil expressed a similar motivation. The director of the Manchete News Network, Zevi Ghivelder, gave an example of how his stations covered national elections in neighbouring Argentina. Instead of sending a whole crew to Argentina, which would require at least a reporter, cameraman, soundman and producer, Ghivelder closed a deal with Channel 13-Argentina and only sent the reporter. The reporter selected the images he needed from those already collected by Channel 13 and all that was required was a one-minute standup. Channel 13 provided the producer and crew and whatever else was necessary.

Ghivelder has made the same offer to other *World Report* contributors. '(TV Manchete has) five stations in Brazil so there is quite a scope in the country,' he said. 'Sometimes you want to cover some items in Brazil, but you feel discouraged because of the rising cost of gathering news. Just send one man and we will provide the crew. We will provide production, even transportation and driver. You can satellite feed from our own facilities. The moment we start doing it among us all over the world, we will cut our costs significantly and it will be a major step forward in our press activity'.

He also offered, 'If you need a story from Brazil, just call us over the phone and we will find what it is you need and ship it to you, or send it by satellite, whatever you need, however you want'.

Uncensored reports

In the survey, news organizations were also asked what they liked about the *CNN World Report*. The items most often noted had to do with the large spectrum of world programming made available, the diversity of points of view, the quality of the production and the scripts provided for each story (so that stories could be translated and reworked for local use). They especially liked the outlet it provided them for telling their own story in their own way to outside audiences.

'CNN includes reports from all over the world, especially the Third World countries, which is seldom available in our regular international TV news services,' reports Teledifusao de Macau. 'Moreover, the reports in CNNWR are more in-depth than those provided by international news services'.

One of the unique features of the *World Report* is that CNN promises to run stories exactly as they are contributed so long as the items are prepared in English and are three-minutes or less in length. The respondent from Samoan TV, the engineer who serves as acting station manager, explained 'We like the fact that these reports are run without CNN censorship. We have had to cut one story here (Carnival time in Rio with all of the big, bare, bouncing b...) for local community standards reasons. However, we appreciate finding out what other national communities feel is important. This is quite often different than what the bureau chiefs of NBC, BBC, AP, etc. feel is news'.

Several respondents expressed concern that some items contributed were too self-serving and 'propagandistic'. 'Some items may be a bit farfetched,' says the foreign affairs editor of NRK-Norway, 'but we understand the idea that once *CNN World Report* opens up for a 'speakers corner' like this, it really has to be uncensored. It is a charming supplement to CNN's own news service'.

United Nations Television Service which has hardly missed a newscast, with 230 stories aired as of April 1990, explains, '*CNN World Report* is the only news programme in the US that truely has an international viewpoint. The audience can see different versions of the same story and not be exposed to only the American perspective'.

Nafis Sadik, who directs the United Nations Population Fund, notes 'We are very excited by the possibility which television opens up for spreading international understanding of population problems and what can be done to solve them'. She credits CNN for 'television productions like *The Day of Five Billion*, which was shown in about 130 countries around the world and was viewed by billions of people,' as having helped heighten awareness of the population problem. *CNN World Report* meets the needs of UN agencies, such as the Population Fund, to get their concerns out 'on everyday type of television'.

'The real test for *CNN World Report*,' says Steve Whitehouse, anchor/producer for most of the UNTV stories, 'will be to show the world that it's possible to report the stories of the 1990s and the year 2000 when many of these stories are not going to be the kinds of things which have traditionally been thought of as news'. He says, 'I think the great challenge for (*World Report* contributors) is to bring these stories and make them news, to show people they are news, and show people there are ways of making these things exciting and relevant. The test is, can we bring a new sort of news, new subjects, new perspectives? ... it's something that is going to take a long time to do'.

How do these stations decide what items to forward to CNN? From the survey, the following criteria appear to be those most often cited: does it have news value, is it of international interest, is it a story the local station can cover, and does it reflect the major social, cultural, political, economic events of the week in the home country that deserve attention of a world audience? The latter criterion and international interest were the items most often cited.

An early producer, who served as anchor for Canal 3-Guatamala for several years, wrote a four-page letter in response to the questionnaire and was also interviewed at one of the contributor conferences in Atlanta. In Guatamala, she says, we often hear about the monopoly of the international news broadcasting systems. 'This is a golden opportunity for us, the developing countries, to give our own point of view on social and political matters of our environment. We decided to participate because we can give news from Guatemala to the rest of the world. My boss, the production director, and I select the topics, depending on the importance of the happenings in our country. We have always to take into account the availablity of the visual material, which many times is considered a problem'.

In her view, 'The reports go from very good quality to very bad quality. The problem is mainly due, I think, to the difference in personnel between the countries with different degrees of development. The only solution for this is training'. She compliments CNN for offering training to *World Report* contributors but worries that 'the countries who will send representatives for training are the ones with better economic resources, the ones who (already) have a better quality in their presentation of information. The poor nations, even if they sincerely want to receive training, may not be able to do so because of economic limitations and this may accentuate even more the difference in production quality'.

The news producer from Guatamala was of the opinion that *World Report* content could be improved by unifying its presentation with respect to subject matter. 'We have seen that the staff of CNN (in Atlanta) are separating the material according to the main subjects. But even so, sometimes the themes are so different that *CNN World Report* turns into an enumeration of reports instead of a unified programme'. She suggests 'the countries of the region could agree on a subject several weeks ahead (giving) their particular country's point of view on a specific happening in the region. Central America has one team, the Middle East has another ... talking about family planning, water supply, foreign debt, etc'.

'I think we all would appreciate a general increase in direction from CNN. In order to improve our own work and, in consequence, the quality of the programme, we would welcome with open arms some written criticisms of our material that would serve us as feedback and an orientation to improve our material'. She re-emphasizes that '*CNN World Report* is a good programme, an opportunity for all of us to contribute and to give our own version of our own news, because that's generally what the international news agencies fail to do for us'. She also sees it as 'an opportunity for all of us to be members of a team of pioneers in this type of programme'.

That's our job, says one respondent. It's the job of news editors to make the decisions about what has news value and what doesn't. 'The news items selected,' according to Peoples Television 4-Philippines, 'are usually those we think have the most impact internationally'. It is the 'local flavor' and the 'unbiased reports from each contributor' that impressed the staff of TV 4 with the *World Report*. 'The programme as a whole is very well-produced and crafted,' PTV 4 wrote, 'and does us proud to be part of the production'.

'The *World Report* provides us with stories which we would not have otherwise,' says Japan Cable Television. 'Stories which we could not report ourselves because of lack of personnel, financial support, or time. Selection of reports for the *World Report* is made with two criteria in mind. First they must be interesting to the (mainly US) audience. They must also be about topics which show aspects of Japan that are strictly Japanese'.

'We find the concept of being part of a 'global newscast' exciting, particularly as it is the first of its kind,' wrote the news director of Network 10-Australia. Topics are selected for the *CNN World Report* 'as we would any news story: content, pictures, interest. We don't have a magazine programme so news value is what counts'. ORF-Austria affirms this view. 'The bottom line is news value for an audience whose image of Austria is shaped by Mozart, mountains and Lipizzan horses. Sure it's all of that,' says Eugen Freund, ORF foreign disk reporter, 'but thanks to CNN and the *World Report*, people now also learn that we have corruption, neo-Nazis, war on our borders and dead bodies in the ice ... so much for my contribution to enhance the image of my country in the world,' he says in jest.

In Taiwan, the chief of the Foreign News Section acknowledged 'It is completely up to me to make selections. Usually I choose those topics that are most interesting to me'. He too asked for more direction, more constructive criticism, from CNN.

Broadcaster concerns

Respondents were also given an opportunity to say what they disliked about the *CNN World Report* and to make recommendations for the improvement of the service. Most of the criticisms and recommended changes were aimed at procedural and technical problems relating to implementation of the global news programme rather than its concept. As mentioned earlier, there were concerns about the self-promotional slant given some of the news items. Some stories, according to those filling out the questionnaire, were pointless and trivial and not newsworthy. There were also criticisms of the poor technical quality of some of the reports, the heavy accents, the washed out pictures, the logos and fonts inserted by CNN which had to be edited out for local re-use.

World Report was also complimented for being 'the next best thing to taking a trip to all the countries which contribute'. But the director of News and Current Affairs of the Caribbean Broadcasting Corporation, Barbados, also noted that 'Some of the English is so heavily accented that it's not always easy to understand the commentary. The colour on some of the reports from Eastern Europe appear gray and washed out'. The difficulties Barbados has in producing and delivering its reports to CNN, he says, is that 'We are so busy working on our own news shows and current affairs programmes that the week goes by very quickly and reports which might be appropriate don't get sent because they would be dated'.

From Hong Kong, the CEO of Asia Television Ltd. had these comments. 'At best, CNNWR can give different perspectives on important news stories. The reports may not be totally objective but if balanced by others can work fine. At worst, reports can be pure propaganda and may be no more than selling political ideologies or consumer products'. The main difficulty the Hong Kong station has in producing the reports is lack of staff. 'We are already overworked'. Since the station hadn't at the time of the survey access to satellite transmission 'it takes days for the items to reach Atlanta by air' and 'by the time the CNNWR is aired here the stories are at least a week old'.

From Canal Plus-France, the producer writes 'It is time-consuming as I have a lot of work during the week. I often have to stay late at night to produce the package'. To rewrite the story in English and voice over it takes a long time,' he says. As for using *World Report* material, 'most of the hot news stories have aged and we have already spoken about them or done in-house packages'. He dislikes the fact that 'The reports are fonted with logos and big letters which tends to force us to edit the stories (if we are) to have continuity in our on-air look'. As for recommendations, he says 'Keep up the great relations with so many different contributors from around the world and also ensure the continuity of the quality of the reports'.

'We appreciate the fact that CNNWR reports are not re-edited,' writes the chief editor of Ghana Broadcasting. 'Where two countries are having problems, CNN tries to make available reports from both sides'. Examples noted were the reports regularly aired from Bayrak Television (Turkish North Cyprus) and CyBC (Greek Cyprus), from Lithuanian and Armenian TV as well as from the state broadcaster TSS-Soviet Union and from Namibia, Angola, Mozambique and Zimbabwe as well as SABC-South Africa.

'Sometimes it is hard to find an item that we consider relevant to CNNWR,' the Ghana broadcaster says. 'Many *World Report* stories are not considered as news by us in the strict sense of the word. A story on the renovation of a museum in Cyprus, for example, will not be considered for our news bulletin ... . The technical quality of some of the reports, particularly those from Latin America, leaves much to be desired. Also we find difficulty in transcribing some of the reports where the scripts are not available'. In answer to the question of what could be done to make the service more useful, he recommended that 'if CNN could focus more on political and economic developments worldwide as opposed to socio-cultural issues, the *World Report* would be even more appreciated. Some of the reports are a week or more late. However, with work on the installation of a satellite dish going very fast, this problem will soon be a thing of the past'.

At the time the questionnaire was administered 82 per cent of contributors shipped their news to Atlanta by way of air freight. On the other hand, 73 per cent received the *CNN World Report* package via satellite. The programme came to the remaining stations via shipping. Since 1990, the number of participating stations still unable to receive by satellite has fallen to about a dozen and the number using satellite to feed their stories has markedly increased, although there are still many for whom this technology is beyond their reach.

International usage

Many stations contributing news to *CNN World Report* find little local use for *World Report* material. This situation may have changed somewhat but at the time of the last survey some 30 per cent of participating stations make no use of the programme to which they contribute stories. Fifty two per cent of those responding do use at least a quarter of the material each week, which from a two hour *World Report* package could mean that 30 minutes is used in a single show or that thirty minutes of material is spread out over the local newscasts for that week. Some use individual reports, some use the materials as a source of file or stock video. Only 25 per cent use *CNN World Report* as a separate programme. Twenty six per cent of those using *World Report* aired the show immediately: 37 per cent aired the show at a later date. Thirty seven per cent of those using the CNN-distributed news indicated the material is translated and subtitled or translated and dubbed. Very likely actual use of *World Report* stories on local stations is less than indicated by the percentages given since those answering the questionnaires are likely to be those who appreciate the programme.

YLE-Finland is an example of a station that has contributed 155 news stories to the weekend and 17 to the daily *World Report*, yet uses none of its material back home. 'As much as I would like to say we have a commitment to hearing other voices, there doesn't seem to be room to use stories (from *World Report*) from Ethiopia and Czechoslovakia and such places,' explains Petri Sarvana, a YLE journalist. He notes that channel space and staff are limited. 'I am pessimistic about using it in the near future'. To make a special programme with its own philosophy needs two full-time translators and additional staff. He also explains that '[YLE] news editors have worked hard to establish their independence and neutrality. It is a basic rule that we don't screw up our credibility with a one-sided peice from Afghanistan. *World Report* just is not as credible as Visnews'.

Within SBC-Singapore, *CNN World Report* is not seen as a principal source for international news, but as an alternative. Chow How Fang of SBC says these stories are 'not really of interest to our audience. We use selected items, one or two per programme. Sometimes we have a little time left and slip one in. Indonesian visual news is hard to get, so we used their drug story'. Individual items aired on SBC normally appear in the half-hour show *World This Week* which airs on Sunday afternoons. Items used are usually those contributed by neighbouring countries within the ASEAN region.

The special problem that SBC faces is that news must be presented in four different languages: English, Mandarin, Malay and Tamil. SBC journalist Bhagman Singh explained that the language problem is also troublesome when collecting the news. He will typically go out and do the story first in English and bring it back and give it to one of the other language services. Since Singaporeans are a multi-lingual population, Singh may ask the persons interviewed to do the response in more than one language. This creates a big rush in trying to get stories ready for airing.

In 1989, TSS-Soviet Union started to use a lot of *CNN World Report* material. Perhaps as much as 80 per cent of the half-hour show *World in a Week* was drawn from the CNN exchange. Many of these stories were aired without change or editorial comment. According to Aleksey Denisov, a TSS journalist interviewed while in a training programme at CNN, the availability of these materials provided an advantage for his station. It was the most objective way they had for covering events. 'We use a lot from Asia, Australia and Latin America, sometimes as a substitute for Visnews, sometimes as a complement,' he said. 'Sometimes the pictures are taken off and used with our own commentary'. Denisov gave as an example a CNN report on drugs, from which TSS made a Soviet version on Soviet drug problems comparing the two.

According to Denisov, CNN was the first American network to sell its programmes in the Soviet Union. His prediction was 'It will help us change things more quickly'. CNN is not a strong competition, he says, because not everybody knows English and people like the established programmes but it is 'a logical step to give us more information from abroad, a way to compare news'.

The best years at TSS, Soviet Central Television, were the years 1988 to 1990, says Peter Orlov, writer-reporter for the *TSS Morning* show. Orlov resigned his position in 1991 and asked to be re-assigned to cover space and science, which he considers a less political job. 'We could report freely, about strikes, drugs, Eastern Europe,' he reminisced about the glasnost years. 'We discussed all these things openly'.

At the time of the attempted coup in August 1991, Soviet Central television had 20,000 employees with its signals covering 93 per cent of the country with five television channels. With the emergence of independent and semi-independent republics, and the privatization of television, it is unclear whether any central television news service will survive, or how CNN will fit in. Stations in Armenia, Estonia, Latvia and Lithuania, have continued contributing, as have some new ones, including Yerevan TV, Ostankino – Russia and Russian TV Channel 1.

Contributors from the former Soviet Union must feel very much as did the repondent from Radioteleviziunea Romania. In a long letter sent along with the returned survey, he wrote, 'It is comforting to notice that there is some interest in the way my organization and myself try to contribute reports from this part of the world, especially at a time when Romania has unjustly such a bad reputation abroad, mainly in the United States'. In the letter he apologized for the fact that Romanian Television was feeding reports to the *CNN World Report* but not using it in return. 'Lack of technical facilities prevent us to use CNNWR, although I think it would be met with great interest by our viewers'.

Deutsche Welle-Germany uses none of the *World Report* material it receives in exchange for its contributions. Although a regular contributor, Deutsche Welle 'cannot make use of CNNWR as we only produce reports from Germany for external broadcasting,' says Siegfried Berndt, director of television. Like the USA's *Voice of America* and *Worldnet* programmes, Deutsche Welle TV does not broadcast in its own country.

Similarly, United Nations Television notes that 'Since the U.N. does not operate a TV station it can only use CNNWR as raw footage'. The *CNN World Report* does provide the U.N. with 'a good outlet for its three-minute programmes called *UN in Action*'. As noted earlier, United Nations Television participates because it is 'a virtually unique way of reaching an informed audience both in the US and elsewhere. Also it is seen in a lot of newsrooms' and '(we) like to support and encourage endeavours which bring the widest possible range of viewpoints to TV'.

CNN World Report has in the meantime responded to some of the recommendations for changes. The staff has worked to encourage regional arrangments so an increased number of contributors can up-link their stories by satellite directly to Atlanta and CNN has itself expanded the reach of its global satellite network. Some technical problems have been overcome to provide two-channel audio with one track devoted to international sound on its satellite out-feeds and, on certain of its satellites, sub-carriers capable of transmitting, along with the video, a data package consisting of scripts and fonts of each news show. What this means is that the local stations will find it easier to re-voice news pieces in the local language and the mailing of scripts and cassettes will be less necessary.

Participating news organizations clearly view the CNN affiliation to be in their interest. They like the openness of the arrangement, which permits them to contribute what they like, when they like. Each contributor has a slightly different reason for participating. This is certainly one of the secrets of *World Report* success. Contributors feel fairly treated by CNN and appreciate the international exposure. They almost all have positive feelings about the need for a Hyde Park-type channel, such as *World Report*, that will air uncensored whatever diverse views there are. Not many of them are willing or are able, for one reason or another, to air much of this material on their own stations.

Reference

1. Helmut Markwort, *Gong*, March 1988.

Chapter 6 EXPANDING THE WORLD NEWS AGENDA

'The most closed societies are now open as a result of television. A new world culture is emerging'.

M.H. Rao, Director of News, Pakistan TV

During the Persian Gulf crisis, whenever George Bush addressed the American people or gave a press conference in Washington he could be sure Saddam Hussein was somewhere out there in the audience. Whatever he said, Bush knew, Hussein would overhear. It was like giving a press release to the enemy. Likewise, when Saddam Hussein supplied broadcasters with pictures of himself at prayer, or made available footage of himself meeting with his commanders in the field – relaxed, smiling, giving encouragement – and when he invited in international correspondents to see for themselves how well he was treating the 'guests' he had taken as hostages when he occupied Kuwait, he knew those images would be replayed throughout the world.

At the very moment both sides were making points about how futile it was trying to understand the other, it is interesting to note that Saddam Hussein and George Bush were relying on the same sources for news of the other, and that Hussein was no less adept than Bush when it came to using the likes of CNN. In courting the CNN cameras, Saddam Hussein showed he knew enough about the way the modern world works to try to make television work for him. The irony is that he found himself endorsing before the world an institution of the West he would never have permitted to be freely seen in Iraq.

In a globally interdependent world with crumbling national and regional frontiers, information is the most precious product of the post-modern economy. The need for information does not respect geography or ideology. Hussein was a political adversary, but he was also a willing consumer of the same news everybody else was watching. As an ideological opponent, he condemned Americans and their institutions; as a head of state and decision-maker, he bought the product that met his needs, even if it was the enemy who was better at assembling it.

Ironically, as far as news is concerned, Saddam Hussein could get an inside look into the American mind that Bush never could have with respect to Arabs and Iraqis. The American-collected news not only provided Hussein with an accounting of the 'facts' concerning his adversary but there were also clues, cultural lessons to be learned, about how the enemy thought and why the enemy thought as it did. For the Iraqi leader, keeping an eye on the international news was a form of reconnaisance, revealing a great deal about the assumptions, understandings, aspirations and resolve of those who stood against him.

Television diplomacy

Americans, and Europeans as well, pay the penalty for dominating international news; they lose the chance to learn how others think. It's not that American news reporters don't cover events in other lands. They do, but they cover them selectively and from the perspective of what the viewers back home want to see. The aftermath of the Gulf conflict demonstrates this. Americans were mystified (and some quite upset) that there were critics questioning the way the Allies managed the war, a war that from the average United States citizen's point of view was a noble, principled and unselfish undertaking. Having followed closely the unfolding events on TV, where news cameras gave their near-exclusive attention for a month, it was simply incomprehensible to Americans that others could see those same events differently.

Nimer Al-Adwan, Jordan TV news anchor, is one of those quick to indict CNN along with the rest of the American media when it comes to bias in its coverage of the Middle East. 'I see CNN as an extension of American foreign policy,' he says. '(CNN) doesn't cover the whole issue, only from the point of view of what is of interest to Americans'. In the Gulf crisis, he insists, the American media only covered what the adminstration wanted it to cover.

The accusation that the American media are pawns of the US government is another of those imponderables. How could this be true in America? Surely not. Yet, there's certainly something to it, for where US interests lie, the media are sure to follow. And the obverse is also true. Where the Secretary of State does not travel, the press do not go either. What the White House fails to notice, more often than not, the TV cameras are certain to ignore as well. Instead of offering up the agenda, our journalists spend their time following whatever agenda the White House sets. In the way of explanation, they say it's a matter of priority, and it's what the American people want.

During the Persian Gulf crisis, while Allied Forces were intent on forcing Iraq to withdraw from Kuwait, the American-based pressure group Accuracy in Media had a national campaign going aimed at forcing CNN to withdraw from Iraq. Expressing outrage, AIM claimed that CNN had 'put its facilities at the disposal of a ruthless dictator with whom this country is at war'. Three weeks into the seige, CNN acknowledged it had received 36,000 telephone calls, 15,000 letters and 3460 faxes, most of them critical of its coverage of the war. CNN's official position was, 'The viewer responses have not affected our editorial decision-making process. We make our decisions on what's important and newsworthy'.

Tom Johnson, who left a job as publisher of the *Los Angeles Times* to become president of CNN, arrived for work 24 hours before Iraq invaded Kuwait on August 2, 1991. He found himself in the thick of the controversy, a controversy that put to the test CNN's credibility as a world-class broadcaster. To those who would have CNN assist in securing US interests in the Gulf, he had this to say, 'We have been told that to allow Saddam

Hussein or his spokesmen uninterrupted and unedited access to our air is wrong. Yet, they raise no objections when we've telecast uninterrupted and unedited speeches by President Bush, Prime Minister Thatcher, Prime Minister Mulroney, the chairman of the Joint Chiefs of Staff and many others'.

'Let me be very blunt,' he says. 'Our goal at CNN is neither to assist, nor to inhibit the dipolmats of any country as they seek a solution for this, or any other crisis. It is our goal to provide fair and balanced reporting of all news and all views that are relevant to the events of the day. Certainly, some US diplomats may wish we did not reveal Saddam Hussein's arguments to the rest of the world. And Iraqi diplomats may wish that we did not let President Bush make his case to the international community. But diplomats aside, all of us can only benefit from this open access to information'.

'I get the sense that some of those who slammed CNN for airing the two Iraqi broadcasts in their entirety did so because they felt Mr. Hussein might pull the wool over the eyes of the viewing audience, that their editors were a better judge of propaganda than the public we all serve. Well, we at CNN don't think we have to protect our audience from so-called propaganda. We think our viewers can look at a lengthy appearance by Saddam Hussein – or George Bush for that matter – and make up their minds about what it means'.

Viewer concerns, and especially those of pressure groups, do make broadcasters nervous, not because viewers spend less time viewing but because they might not buy the products advertisers are trying to sell. Advertisers don't like wars anyway, because they interrupt the schedule and run the risk of associating their products with bad news. In the Persian Gulf war American broadcasters actually had to absorb the enormous add-on costs, estimated at US$150 million for the four US networks, running costly 'make-goods' when regular programmes were pre-empted, and practically begging sponsors to bear with them until things were sorted out in the Middle East. The real question for future wars is whether news organizations will show up at all. No matter how morally resolute is the broadcaster and how steadfast is the newsroom in sticking to what it thinks is 'important and newsworthy,' in a commercial broadcasting environment those who decide what will be and will not be covered have to take pressure groups, advertisers and the audience 'back home' into consideration, else the organization itself will falter.

Lest the reader be misled, newsrooms are not necessarily less constrained in countries where commercial advertisement has less influence. What is news in a one-party state is likely to be a government decision made in the name of the people but with little concern for what does not correspond to official positions. News programming may reflect viewer interests but more likely the medium is there to instruct, command and exhort the public for its own good. Viewers are not expected to influence content when others in a better position to know what is best have been appointed to make those decisions.

There are those who argue that development communication – communications for the public good – is not journalism but public relations, propaganda and selling. There are others who argue that there can be no journalism without social reponsibility, that a free and commercial market in news leaves entire societies under-represented and important issues unaddressed. In light of evidence that Western news organizations do tend to give their international attention to politics and conflict and concentrate their resources on the roving 'hot spots,' and that the developing countries will persist in using the media to protect and perpetuate governments in power and selectively promote issues they consider important, there seems no reconciling the two.

Developing countries need the media to help achieve their national goals. When governments identify problems of inflation, population or pollution and set out to resolve such matters as ethnic tension and racial strife within the country, what is wrong in using the national media to motivate citizens to support those efforts? When there are policies in need of explaining and concerns that must be aired to other countries, what is wrong in bringing to bear national media resources for that purpose? The mass media, then, becomes a player in the government's plans. From the point of view of national interests, this is a more acceptable and socially responsible role for the media to play than merely selling consumer goods because it is for the benefit of the country and all its citizens.

Of course, in the developed world, this view goes against the grain, for it requires a different understanding of the role of government and the press. News media touting the party line, or 'getting on the team,' as US correspondents in Vietnam were exhorted to do, assumes that the government has the public's best interest at heart. The inherent danger in 'government say-so' communication is that there often is no checks-and-balances, thus is open to abuse. The market-driven system at least saves the media from having to run unwatched programmes just because some government office thinks they 'ought' to be there.

CNN has seemingly found in *World Report* a way to avoid getting captured by one or the other of these camps. *World Report* is a commercial product which can live with the fact that some of the news it airs has a promotional quality to it and that some of its news is collected from a perspective a majority of viewers will not agree with. Independent of the argument of whether there is such a thing as 'neutral' or 'objective' news, the self-defined goal of *World Report* is to present as many points of view as there are. The special mission of *World Report* is to put its effort into increasing the number of news-contributing nations, wherever possible giving voice to those not normally heard, and seeing that for every perspective – whether from the South or North, East or West – each has an equal chance of being heard. This it sees as its social responsibility.

Alternative news

Analysis of *World Report* content shows that domestic relations and foreign affairs are categories of news given most frequent attention. Economics and ecology are also topics of broad concern. Racial/ethnic relations, social services, education and religion are further down on the list of news priority. Except for an increased amount of cultural-type programmes, all these categories of news are similar in frequency of appearance to those of the other international services. What is different perhaps, that the statistical tabulations do not show, is the perspective on the topic, in many cases the giving of multiple perspectives on the same event. In effect, *World Report* is there not to give a neutral and objective report on the BCCI bank scandal, but to allow CRTV-Cameroon and KTN-Kenya to tell the world how the collapse of this bank has affected the people they represent, a perspective American viewers would otherwise never get.

World Report is there so that YRTV-Republic of Yemen may call attention to the fact that more than one million Yemeni workers returned home from jobs in Kuwait and Saudi Arabia. These workers are no longer sending pay checks to their families in Yemen, causing an income loss for the families and affecting the overall economy of Yemen. The value of such a report is that it illustrates a result of the Persian Gulf war which would have likely escaped the notice of Western viewers and perhaps Yemen's own neighbours.

World Report is there so that TV Asahi-Japan can explain to those who have forgotten or who never realized that Japan was prohibited constitutionally from maintaining an offensive military force, the reason why its military contribution to Operation Desert Storm was minimal. And it is there so that President Mubarak of Egypt can call on the international community to create a Middle East nuclear-free zone. Interviewed in a report submitted by ETV-Egypt, Mubarak pointed out that all five of the United Nations Security Council members appear at the top of the list in international arms sales. Would Western journalists have raised such an issue? Perhaps.

YLE-Finland, proud of the fact that in a survey of 30 nations Finland ranked number one in providing the best living conditions for women, featured this accomplishment in its report to CNN. The report pointed out that Finland had been the first European country to allow the political participation of women and that, in 1991, 50 per cent of the Finnish workforce is made up of women. Forty per cent of the government posts are held by women. This good news story would possibly have made its way into US homes anyway, perhaps not.

Widening the eye of the camera, then, is a contribution *World Report* makes to international news coverage. In a sense, *World Report* is CNN's answer to the thinking viewer's question, 'What is *not* news?' Journalism research shows that, in general, what is not news in commercial broadcasting is either what is perceived to have low viewer interest, what is thought to be too costly or difficult to collect, or there's no time to show. If it's not conflict, it's not news. If it's about people and places the US public does not care about, or have a special connection to, the US media won't give it coverage. If the story is not covered from the US point of view (or at least by one of the established credible sources such as British Broadcasting Corporation, Independent Television News, World Television News or Visnews), it's not aired. These are the simplified conclusions of quantitative research, but such predispositions are clearly present in the news business and over the long run they do have an effect.

World Report is the experiment which tests public interest in stories from wherever, in stories collected by reporters viewers may have never heard of, presenting points of view with which they may not agree. These are stories in which Vietnamese, Cubans, Russians, Syrians and white South Africans can be 'the good guys' for a change. There can be a string of stories in which not a single catastrophy is mentioned. More time is given to the presentation of what is news world-wide and opportunity is given to air exactly those items which, in the day-to-day judgements of time-pressed gatekeepers of established agencies, are less than pressing priority.

In July 1991, there was an Ibero-American summit held in Mexico attended by the nations of Central and South America and the Caribbean. In terms of US relations with its southern neighbours and in terms of Latin nations' relationships with each other, this event had the potential to be one of the important events in recent history. It went almost unnoticed by American television, including CNN. The Ibero-American summit had the poor timing to be scheduled opposite a Bush-Gorbachov meeting in Moscow on strategic arms reduction and a presumed breakthrough in the Israel-Palestenian problem. *World Report* viewers at least got a chance to see English language coverage of the event from the perspective of TV Manchete-Brazil and ICRT-Cuba.

Reciprocal news

Turning on the news, for most of us, is the only way of seeing and hearing what is too far away to witness personally. The evening news is our way of visiting, of taking a quick trip – sometimes for fun, sometimes when we have a real need to know – to places that are otherwise remote, inaccessible and of little interest. Implicit in the *World Report* programme is the assumption that nations of the world will get along better if they share their experience, give voice to their concerns, teach each other. This is a Ted Turner principle, that news is best when it is not all one-way, when we can learn from one another. He says, 'you let people say what they have to say but air the other side' as well.

Iraq was in fact making an effort to tell its side of the story all along. There just were no international channels available with which it could do that. When CNN in 1987 initiated its global newscast, all the Middle Eastern countries with television news organizations, including Iraq, Iran, Jordan, Israel, Saudi Arabia and Kuwait were invited as contributors. Over time, most of them decided to participate. Iraqi TV, in November 1988, submitted a story on a meeting of the Baath Party convened by Saddam Hussein to express support for Palestinians. Such stories gave Western viewers their first opportunity to learn by means of mainstream TV about the Middle East from the point of view of those who live there. At the time, since mainstream TV had not called it to their attention, American viewers were unaware of why they should take notice.

For most of us, unless our news people tell us to pay attention, we don't. In the case of Iraq we in America didn't get involved until we suddenly discovered that 500,000 US troops were being sent there. That got our attention. Then we watched to figure out what it was all about.

Nothing breaks geographic distance like television, or introduces people to each other quicker. TV has that visceral, visual and aural immediacy which can put us right under the table with Bernard Shaw in a Baghdad hotel the first night of the bombing and transport us right to the site of the air-raid shelter from which charred bodies were being removed following an Allied surgical strike. Or alternatively, to keep us at a distance so that we might very well conclude after the war is over that nobody got hurt. We have to keep reminding ourselves that the window that TV opens is a particular perspective, a point from which we as viewers stand and look in or out, a limited frame.

Although writers like to use the 'window on the world' metaphor, what is characteristic of windows is that they allow some things to be seen clearly and others to remain hidden. The angle of view and what the window frames makes a difference in the telling of the story. This is the nature of television news.

In times of international crisis, people count on television news for the most direct and credible representation of reality possible. Given television's power of legitimation, the picture it paints is likely to be our final and authoritative image when it comes to arriving at a satisfying picture of those distant people we now have a need to understand. When alternative channels of information are few and there is no way to access those people and their cultures directly, the TV portrait – no matter how sketchy – is the one we will trust. Indeed, experimental studies have shown that even when audiences tend to question the reliability of news coverage at home, they are much more willing to accept the fairness of our own news coverage abroad.

After all, there is nothing in our experience to prove the news fragmentary, selective, partial or inadequate in its approach. In the absence of contrast such pictures from abroad become all-encompassing and absolute. The way our newsrooms present it to us is 'the way it must be,' for they are the professionals we have trusted with this kind of work. But this global system of information, centred on the industrialized West, imposes on the rest of the world a political and cultural marginalization. As we of the West are frequently reminded, the picture we have of those abroad is skewed, self-serving and full of stereotypes. Hardly ever does Lithuania get to report about Lithuania, Cuba about Cuba, the PLO about Palestine, the Afghans, Tamils, Turks and Greek Cypriots to report on each other, which leaves the international audience with only American or European-centred perspectives on what is going on in the world.

The culprit is not just the reporter and the news agency, rather it is the lop-sided way international reporting is done and the lack of alternatives. Typically, those countries that do not belong to the sphere of the First World do not report, they are reported upon. Their news events are collected and aired through agencies that are, for the most part, culturally grounded in the West. Latin American countries have traditionally had to go to American information sources to know what is happening with their own neighbours. Still today, Africa knows of Asia and Asia of Africa mainly through sources originating in Western Europe.

When the places being reported on are geographically and culturally remote, what is chosen as exceptional and noteworthy for news coverage tends to be in the absence of knowing what is typical and normal. The folks at home see the images of Armenia on TV, or Liberia, Namibia, Nicaragua and Quatar, with few referents as to what constitutes everyday life in those places. Given the lack of something concrete with which to contrast these images, the exceptional becomes the daily norm, the dysfunctional becomes expected and what the reporter judges to be newsworthy becomes the standing reality.

Inclusive news

Within American journalism there are at least three distinct schools of thought when it comes to good journalistic practice. The traditional approach is for journalists to look for the facts and work to get these out as quickly and as accurately as possible. What the journalist has to worry about is telling the story as it happened, letting the news elements judge the value of the story. A second perspective on news reporting is to go beyond the facts to seek out their underlying causes and their implications. News has to be reported in context to insure the right meaning comes through. Interpretation is involved so the reporter has to worry about getting the complete picture of what is going on. This means the journalist has to pay attention to what is left out, what the facts of the case do not say.

A third perspective – one which makes some Western newspeople uncomfortable – is to view journalists basically as activists. News is a means of improving society and achieving justice. Such reporting requires courage and caring since on the one hand the reporter may have to tell his/her story ignoring its effect on advertisers and controlling boards while on the other hand recognizing that what is reported and the way it is reported can have life or death consequences on those affected.

Westerners have been coached into believing that news is objective and that the definition of 'professional' in reporting is to be neutral. Books have been written about whether or not such is possible but, clearly, to report events is to choose some images and not others, to select some people for interviews and to leave others out. As far as Turner Broadcasting is concerned, an educative function is being played by the media whether we admit it or not, whether we like it or not. The problem is that the education provided by commercial broadcasters is not always the one you would like to pass on to your children. Thus, Turner's decision to use his position as international broadcaster to set a more positive global agenda. He knows, in an open society, he may not have the ability to shape how people think about environmental and peace issues but he can at least put those issues before the public to think about. In the textbooks it's called socially responsibile broadcasting.

It is well-known that Turner has a profit agenda but, at the same time, doesn't mind being thought of as a 'do-gooder'. If, in informing the public, international tensions can be lowered, stereotypes eliminated and the environment improved, so much the better. Barbara Pyle, Turner's vice president for environmental policy, calls it 'putting the vision back into television'.

Pyle, who is responsible for TBS's animated cartoon *Captain Planet*, says, 'The communications industry is the only instrument that has the capacity to educate on a scale needed, in the time available'. Her show *Captain Planet and the Planeteers*, as she explains, is a children's action adventure cartoon which casts five children from five corners of the earth (Africa, Asia, Latin America, Eastern Europe and North America) to work together as a team to tackle environmental and peace issues. Twenty six half-hour episodes have been produced. These are shown on the TBS cable channels and marketed in several languages around the world.

'What we've managed to accomplish is not only to make the programmes very very entertaining, but they are also educational. But you don't really feel that they're educational because they're so much fun that adults actually learn from these episodes as well as children,' she says. 'After you've watched one of these episodes you will understand. Say, for the episode about the ozone hole, you will definitely understand the relationship between CFCs and ozone depletion. And these issues aren't easy and to be able to make them easy to understand in cartoon form – as my boss says, 'A problem recognized is a problem half solved'. And this is our goal in this programme: for us to be able to recognize the problems. And our other goal is for us to be able to create a global team, to be able to think about and solve these problems'.

The activist perspective assumes that the mass media, by its choice of programming, determines the issues the public thinks and talks about. When the media play up an issue or cover an event, the public eventually comes to regard that issue/event as significant. The opposite is also true. When the media do not pay attention to persons, places, occasions, those cannot be long viewed as important. Socially reponsible broadcasting means that broadcasters have to be conscious of more than profit, they have to be conscious of what view of the world their audiences will come away with as a result of what they choose or chose not to show them.

Turner has gone further. He not only has his own view of the way the world ought to be, he believes others should be able to express their own view as well, even when those views conflict with his. *World Report* is Turner's own affirmative action programme for world news intended to correct what are now long-standing imbalances. Perhaps Turner's lasting contribution will be seen not in having sent out news crews to address unaddressed issues but in having encouraged local broadcasters to cover the news however they see it, and to provide a channel by which collected stories can be aired globally.

World Report does not presume to predefine what news is, nor does it assume that all news should be handled the same way. *World Report* takes stories that mirror events as they occur, it takes reflective pieces which give background and provide interpretation and it takes stories with an agenda created especially to leave an impression or move the audience to some action. What CNN provides is the structure into which news of whatever type can fit.

What has emerged in *World Report* is a type of newscast the world has never before seen and an audience no newservice has ever before felt called upon to address. This world audience, in spite of its cultural differences, sits before a concert of global reporters, savoring the multiple points of view, those of 'our side,' those of 'the enemy' and those whom in our busy lives we would have forgotten are still there. It is up to the viewer to sort through and decide what it all means.

It does not follow inevitably that such a diversity of views will lead to greater understanding and a lessening of conflict in the world. Saddam Hussein had access to world news and got from it what he wanted to hear. Seeing the protests in the streets and the debates in the US Congress arguing that the US should stay out of Middle Eastern affairs, he perhaps concluded that he was up against a divided enemy. Having no experience with democracy, so many points of view so openly aired may have led him to conclude there was a lack of unity, a lack of resolve in the coalition forming against him. In an open society television collects and makes the voices available but it doesn't have to tell viewers what to make of what they see. As television increasingly becomes the language of international culture, will *CNN World Report* be the model to follow? Our conclusion: if it is not the model we had better hope it is part of the mix.

Reference

1. Doug Halonen, 'Coalition Fights to Stop CNN's Coverage,' *Electronic Media*, February 8, 1991.

Chapter 7   CONCLUSIONS

'Our heritage stories, our Christmas celebrations, are at the bottom of our priorities'.
Milan Tomanek, Journalist, Czechoslovakian Television, 1991

When Ted Turner got it in his mind that there should be a place in international news where 'everybody in the world has the opportunity to speak to everybody else in the world on a regular basis,' he gave it to the staff at CNN to work out. The problem the staff faced was not just the details of how to do this, who to invite, what conditions to set, how to get the news to Atlanta and what sort of format to adopt in inaugurating what would become the world's first communal newscast. The CNN staff had to insure such an undertaking would not undermine the company's credibility as an international news service.

The *World Report* venture raised red flags all over the place. News arriving in Atlanta from contributors was of variable quality, large chunks of it technically unacceptable by Western standards. The stories were boring and didn't always make sense; the heavily accented English was difficult to follow. But what was more worrisome, the content could not be trusted. CNN had given up editorial control. There were calls and letters praising Turner's courage but there were letters that said, 'Shame on you, CNN. *World Report* is nothing more than a forum for the world's propaganda mills'.

Five years have passed. Some 8000 news stories have been aired on the weekend and 2000 items have run on the daily World Reports. Broadcast news organizations from 130 countries have contributed news. What can be concluded about the accommodations CNN has made to this innovation in news? What benefits has this service brought and what impact, if any, has it had on the distribution and use of internationally-collected news abroad?

Internal acceptance

CNN World Report was clearly struggling in its early years. It struggled to find its identity, it struggled to create a somewhat-standard operating procedure, it struggled to gain acceptance within CNN itself and it struggled to prove that it needed resources and staff to make the idea work. There were no ready models to look to, nothing similar with which it could be easily compared. *World Report* was basically all new territory in the international news business.

Being accepted 'on the news side' – as it is referred to within CNN – was a big step forward for *World Report*, for that meant it was not just a programme segment in the CNN schedule, it was a part of CNN's newsgathering strategy. In hot spots, such as the Commonwealth of Independent States, *World Report* contributors have begun filing their perspectives live from CNN bureaus abroad. In places such as South Korea, bureau heads have begun encouraging local broadcasters to take greater advantage of the *World Report* outlet for their news. *World Report* contributors in places like India and Yugoslavia are used as sources for news on the network. This rarely happened earlier.

Quality control

CNN took several steps to get control over the quality and timeliness of the product and to make the newscast more appealing. *World Report* training programmes and the staff's on-going 'TV correspondence course' helped the less-experienced broadcasters improve their writing, editing, interviewing skills and proper use of the English language.

Attention was given the look of the show. Money was spent on a special studio set, special graphics were developed, the pace was quickened (in June 1991, the maximum length of *World Report* stories was reduced from three to two-and-a-half minutes) and communications with contributors and advance planning were given a staff priority. Although still set off from network news programming by distinctive graphics and set, and anchor disclaimers ('bringing you perspectives from the world's broadcasters ...'.) are written into every show, the overall effect is to make *World Report* news look more like regular CNN news.

Hard news

Like CNN regular news, *World Report* staff have moved to generate more timely news. The daily *World Report* is the focus of this change but its spin-off is felt in the weekend programme as well. Much of the incentive for tuning in to CNN, the staff say, is to find out what is going on at the moment. There is room for the softer features but 'hot news' is popular with the kind of audience to which CNN appeals. Weekend *World Report* newscasts now open with the breaking news stories of the week, if not the breaking news of that very hour.

Although *World Report* editors do not control the content of what participating broadcasters send them, they do decide where stories are positioned in the newscast. Traditionally, the lead story in any newscast is a signal to the audience that they are witnessing the most important story of the day. This pattern has been followed by the staff at *World Report*, except their leads will not always mimic those of the other networks, or even of CNN itself.

In February 1991, the entire first half-hour of the *World Report* was devoted to non-Persian Gulf war news. This occurred at a time when all eyes were on the Middle East as the Allied Forces were poised to begin a ground offensive on the heels of a furious bombardment of Iraq and numerous peace initiatives. Almost as if to remind the world that life was going on elsewhere, the *World Report* newscast led with stories on the independence movements in the Baltics, the trial of Winnie Mandela in South Africa, the impact of rising fuel prices in Zambia, Mozambique and Zimbabwe and international relief operations in Ethiopia. (Note: The producer of this *World Report* show was called in for a 'consultation' afterwards with CNN news bosses. Apparently, her explanation satisfied them that she had made an acceptable decision.)

As the message gets out that it's hard news CNN wants to see, the pressure will be off journalists to do 'development news'. Development news is given lower priority especially when there are so many crises to report, which may account for the research showing the greater proportion of non-crisis news now being submitted by the more developed countries.

Agenda-setting

More control is being taken with *World Report* content. Increasingly, requests for stories around a theme are being made of contributors, so that at least one newscast a month either is a special programme or carries a special segment. These themes, such as antiquities preservation, refugees and homeless, Persian Gulf anniversary reports, women and the environment, are attempts to give the programme focus, impact and viewer appeal.

The *World Report* newscast has thus become less pot-luck. Contributors are no less free to decide whether or not to contribute, to decide what they will say or the angle given their stories, and all reports will still be aired no matter the topic, but a stronger hand has been taken in setting the agenda. Such changes seem to be welcomed by contributors and viewers alike.

If the full diversity of *World Report* is being patted into a shape that looks more like Western TV, no one seems to be complaining. CNN is riding a wave of popularity envied by newscasters everywhere. Contributors to *World Report* are genuinely pleased to have their work appear on the CNN network and when their reports come up to 'the CNN standard,' they get only compliments from viewers back home.

Access to news

To cover the news internationally, news organizations must be at the right place at the right time with the means to get their stories back to news centre. Part of the reason CNN has been able to do timely reporting from China, Yugoslavia, South Africa, Libya, wherever and whenever the story is breaking, has been its credibility going in as a 'fair and balanced' newscaster. The other part has been the work it has done building its base of contacts in the world news community. Personal relationships with local broadcasters around the world, over an extended period of time, have given it unusual visibility, acceptance and access. This may or may not have been a part of the rationale for inaugurating *World Report*, but it certainly works in CNN's favour now.

Further accommodations

CNN has apparently discovered, through *News Hound* (man on the street with home video camera) stories and through *World Report*, the public will accept less-than-perfect pictures and sound on TV if the content is compelling. On-site footage of a man being beaten by officers of the Los Angeles police department or an aborted coup in the Soviet

Union or the asassination of a world leader, such as Rajiv Gandhi, will attract viewers no matter the quality of the pictures.

Likewise, since CNN aspires to be more than a domestic broadcaster carrying American-oriented reports filed from a foreign dateline, CNN is airing reports not prepared in standard American-English, or even BBC-English for that matter. Americans rarely speak a second language, are not used to hearing other languages spoken and are impatient with accents. *CNN World Report* may be helping to move those audiences into the global community. In the future, it will be less and less likely home audiences can expect to view only news in which cultural differences has been edited out and *World Report* is a glimpse of that future time.

Contributed news

It's more difficult to assess the effect *World Report* is having on international news-gathering, or changes *World Report* may be bringing about in the concept of what is news and who may report it. Looking at *World Report* content, it is obvious there is a huge volume of locally-produced news now being generated that was absolutely unavailable before. That news, coming from an unprecedent number of broadcast news organizations in almost as many countries as there are in the United Nations, represents a diversity unmatched in any other news service. And because that news goes out on the internation-ally distributed CNN channel, it is more widely available.

In general, the news seen on *CNN World Report* is the same old news of the world, namely, domestic and international politics, economics and business news, news of military and defence actions. Environment and ecology, arts and culture, science, health, and social services are news topics that appear more frequently on *World Report* but there is evidence to suggest these topics represent issue shifts around the world, thus are getting greater attention on all news services. The difference is perhaps not the topic but the perspective. A greater number of international news stories are being told from the perspective of those closest to the events, sometimes by those affected personally, as with the reports from Lithuanian TV (its station surrounded by Soviet paratroopers) and JRT-Croatia (its cities being bombed.)

As with international news on other services, the newsmakers tend to be public officials. The number of persons representing academic and scientific fields and those who are ordinary citizens are significantly greater on *World Report*. Women rarely appear as newsmakers, on *World Report* or elsewhere, but women have apparently made signifi-cant inroads as reporters on *World Report*. The number of women reporters contributing stories to *World Report* from stations in Asia and the Middle East is greater than the number of men reporters.

As noted, *World Report* special focus programmes have devoted attention to themes such as abortion, AIDS, environment, homeless, population and religion. These reports have added enormously to the number of stories from an international perspective that address pressing global issues of our time. The *World Report* specials may represent the single most lasting contribution of the news service for they have the impact to influence public policy.

Regional balance

All regions are covered by *World Report* news. Western Europe and Asia are the dominant ones. In the 1990s, the Middle East and Eastern Europe have both come forward in the news, with Africa and Latin America dropping further down. Asia produced more total stories with only the fourth largest number of *World Report* contributors. Latin America and the Caribbean actually had the largest number of news agencies and separate countries contributing, even though they generated the fewest contributions. Whether these imbalances are due to economics or some other reasons, the research does not determine. What is certain, more visual news of the neglected countries, whether from Africa, Latin America, South Pacific, or elsewhere, is being made available to international viewers in one year than will be seen in a decade of coverage on any other service.

Media diplomacy

The prospects for a new information order dimmed when the United States in 1984 pulled out of UNESCO. The Third World especially had looked to UNESCO as the international forum within which to work for a more balanced flow in world news. The issue seemed all but dead when Turner picked it up in 1987.

One of the reasons Turner got the reception he did with *World Report* was that the community of nations, not just the Third World but all nations, were in need of a more public way of talking and explaining themselves to each other. *CNN World Report* provided the medium, excluding noone and placing no restrictions on topic. What has resulted is a kind of international diplomacy network to which most nations of the world now contribute.

Sean MacBride, head of the UNESCO-initiated International Commission for the Study of Communication Problems, wrote in his 1980 report, *Many Voices, One World*, that the goal of the new world information and communication order was 'to replace dependence, dominance and inequality by more fruitful and open relations of inter-dependence and complementarity, based on mutual interest and equal dignity of nations and peoples'.[1]

The goals stated in the UNESCO report, whatever individuals may think of UNESCO itself, serve as a way to measure informally the contributions now being made by the *CNN World Report*. The CNN news service has addressed the equity question, that is, in who may contribute stories for international consumption. It has provided for greater reciprocity in the exchange of news, making more local news available to the international viewer. It has empowered local broadcasters not just to tell stories of local colour but to speak to the issues of the day. What is more, it has been an important demonstration that professional journalists, no matter their political credo or cultural background, can work together to promote the free flow of information so vital to international understanding.

Reference

1. Sean MacBride (ed.), *Many Voices, One World*, Paris: UNESCO, 1980, p. 268.

Media titles available from John Libbey

ACAMEDIA RESEARCH MONOGRAPHS

Satellite Television in Western Europe (revised edition 1992)
Richard Collins
Hardback ISBN 0 86196 203 6

Beyond the Berne Convention
Copyright, Broadcasting and the Single European Market
Vincent Porter
Hardback ISBN 0 86196 267 2

The Media Dilemma:
Freedom and Choice or Concentrated Power?
Gareth Locksley
Hardback ISBN 0 86196 230 3

Nuclear Reactions: A Study in Public Issue Television
John Corner, Kay Richardson and Natalie Fenton
Hardback ISBN 0 86196 251 6

Transnationalization of Television in Western Europe
Preben Sepstrup
Hardback ISBN 0 86196 280 X

The People's Voice: Local Radio and Television in Europe
Nick Jankowski, Ole Prehn and James Stappers
Hardback ISBN 0 86196 322 9

Television and the Gulf War
David E. Morrisson
Hardback ISBN 0 86196 341 5

Contra-Flow in Global News
Oliver Boyd Barrett and Daya Kishan Thussu
Hardback ISBN 0 86196 344 X

CNN World Report: Ted Turner's International News Coup
Don M. Flournoy
Hardback ISBN 0 86196 359 8

Small Nations: Big Neighbour
Roger de la Garde, William Gilsdorf and Ilja Wechselmann
Hardback ISBN 0 86196 343 1

BBC ANNUAL REVIEWS

Annual Review of BBC Broadcasting Research: No XV - 1989
Paperback ISBN 0 86196 209 5

Annual Review of BBC Broadcasting Research: No XVI - 1990
Paperback ISBN 0 86196 265 6

Media titles available from John Libbey

Annual Review of BBC Broadcasting Research: No XV - 1991
Paperback ISBN 0 86196 319 9
Peter Menneer (ed)

BROADCASTING STANDARDS COUNCIL PUBLICATIONS

A Measure of Uncertainty: The Effects of the Mass Media
Guy Cumberbatch and Dennis Howitt
Hardback ISBN 0 86196 231 1

Violence in Television Fiction: Public Opinion and Broadcasting Standards
David Docherty
Paperback ISBN 0 86196 284 2

Survivors and the Media
Ann Shearer
Paperback ISBN 0 86196 332 6

Taste and Decency in Broadcasting
Andrea Millwood Hargrave
Paperback ISBN 0 86196 331 8

A Matter of Manners? – The Limits of Broadcast Language
Edited by Andrea Millwood Hargrave
Paperback ISBN 0 86196 337 7

BROADCASTING RESEARCH UNIT MONOGRAPHS

**Quality in Television –
Programmes, Programme-makers, Systems**
Richard Hoggart (ed)
Paperback ISBN 0 86196 237 0

Keeping Faith? Channel Four and its Audience
David Docherty, David E. Morrison and Michael Tracey
Paperback ISBN 0 86196 158 7

**Invisible Citizens:
British Public Opinion and the Future of Broadcasting**
David E. Morrison
Paperback ISBN 0 86196 111 0

School Television in Use
Diana Moses and Paul Croll
Paperback ISBN 0 86196 308 3

Media titles available from John Libbey

UNIVERSITY OF MANCHESTER BROADCASTING SYMPOSIUM

And Now for the BBC ...
Proceedings of the 22nd Symposium 1991
Nod Miller and Rod Allen (eds)
Paperback ISBN 0 86196 318 0

Published in association with UNESCO

Video World-Wide: An International Study
Manuel Alvarado (ed)
Paperback ISBN 0 86196 143 9

Published in association with
THE ARTS COUNCIL of GREAT BRITAIN

Picture This: Media Representations of Visual Art and Artists
Philip Hayward (ed)
Paperback ISBN 0 86196 126 9

Culture, Technology and Creativity
Philip Hayward (ed)
Paperback ISBN 0 86196 266 4

ITC TELEVISION RESEARCH MONOGRAPHS

Television in Schools
Robin Moss, Christopher Jones and Barrie Gunter
Hardback ISBN 0 86196 314 8

Television: The Public's View
Barrie Gunter and Carmel McLaughlin
Hardback ISBN 0 86196 348 2

The Reactive Viewer
Barrie Gunter and Mallory Wober
Hardback ISBN 0 86196 358 X

REPORTERS SANS FRONTIÈRES

1992 Report
Freedom of the Press Throughout the World
Paperback ISBN 0 86196 369 5

Media titles available from John Libbey

IBA TELEVISION RESEARCH MONOGRAPHS

Teachers and Television:
A History of the IBA's Educational Fellowship Scheme
Josephine Langham
Hardback ISBN 0 86196 264 8

Godwatching: Viewers, Religion and Television
Michael Svennevig, Ian Haldane, Sharon Spiers and Barrie Gunter
Hardback ISBN 0 86196 198 6
Paperback ISBN 0 86196 199 4

Violence on Television: What the Viewers Think
Barrie Gunter and Mallory Wober
Hardback ISBN 0 86196 171 4
Paperback ISBN 0 86196 172 2

Home Video and the Changing Nature of Television Audience
Mark Levy and Barrie Gunter
Hardback ISBN 0 86196 175 7
Paperback ISBN 0 86196 188 9

Patterns of Teletext Use in the UK
Bradley S. Greenberg and Carolyn A. Lin
Hardback ISBN 0 86196 174 9
Paperback ISBN 0 86196 187 0

Attitudes to Broadcasting Over the Years
Barrie Gunter and Michael Svennevig
Hardback ISBN 0 86196 173 0
Paperback ISBN 0 86196 184 6

Television and Sex Role Stereotyping
Barrie Gunter
Hardback ISBN 0 86196 095 5
Paperback ISBN 0 86196 098 X

Television and the Fear of Crime
Barrie Gunter
Hardback ISBN 0 86196 118 8
Paperback ISBN 0 86196 119 6

Behind and in Front of the Screen - Television's Involvement with Family Life
Barrie Gunter and Michael Svennevig
Hardback ISBN 0 86196 123 4
Paperback ISBN 0 86196 124 2